ROYAL NAVY GRAND FLEET 1914–18

Britain's last supreme naval fleet

Angus Konstam
Illustrated by Edouard A. Groult

OSPREY PUBLISHING
Bloomsbury Publishing Plc
Kemp House, Chawley Park, Cumnor Hill, Oxford OX2 9PH, UK
29 Earlsfort Terrace, Dublin 2, Ireland
1385 Broadway, 5th Floor, New York, NY 10018, USA
E-mail: info@ospreypublishing.com
www.ospreypublishing.com

OSPREY is a trademark of Osprey Publishing Ltd

First published in Great Britain in 2025

© Osprey Publishing Ltd, 2025

All rights reserved. No part of this publication may be reproduced or transmitted in any form or by any means, electronic or mechanical, including photocopying, recording, or any information storage or retrieval system, without prior permission in writing from the publishers.

A catalogue record for this book is available from the British Library.

ISBN: PB 9781472866837; eBook 9781472866820; ePDF 9781472866806; XML 9781472866813

25 26 27 28 10 9 8 7 6 5 4 3 2 1

Maps by bounford.com
Diagrams by Adam Tooby
Index by Fionbar Lyons
Typeset by PDQ Digital Media Solutions, Bungay, UK
Printed and bound by Repro India Ltd

Front Cover: Art by Edouard A. Groult, © Osprey Publishing
Osprey Publishing supports the Woodland Trust, the UK's leading woodland conservation charity.

To find out more about our authors and books visit www.ospreypublishing.com. Here you will find extracts, author interviews, details of forthcoming events and the option to sign up for our newsletter.

All photos courtesy of the Stratford Archive.

CONTENTS

INTRODUCTION	4
THE FLEET'S PURPOSE	6
FLEET FIGHTING POWER	12
The Ships	
Technical Factors	
HOW THE FLEET OPERATED	25
Command and Organization	
Intelligence, Communication and Deception	
Bases and Logistics	
COMBAT AND ANALYSIS	56
The Fleet in Combat	
Analysis	
FURTHER READING	79
INDEX	80

INTRODUCTION

The dreadnought HMS *Colossus*, namesake of her class, pictured at anchor in Scapa Flow in the main fleet anchorage off Flotta, looking east. In the background are Bellerophon- and St Vincent-class dreadnoughts and a scattering of light cruisers, with the small Calf of Flotta behind them, while to the right is part of the larger island of Flotta.

In August 1914, at the start of World War I, the bulk of the Royal Navy's battlefleet was combined into a single entity and given the imposing title of 'The Grand Fleet'. It certainly lived up to its name. This was the largest and most modern battlefleet in the world, made up of powerful dreadnought battleships, which collectively possessed a hitherto unimagined level of naval firepower. It was hoped that these dreadnoughts would soon bring their German counterparts to battle and vanquish them in a single great clash of arms. The man placed in charge of this great fleet was Admiral Sir John Jellicoe, a quiet, dignified naval officer who had the intelligence and force of mind to ensure victory.

It had already been decided that in the event of a war with Germany, the battlefleet would be sent north to Scapa Flow in Orkney, a remote but commodious wartime anchorage, beyond the reach of any surprise attack the enemy might launch. There, the fleet was well-placed to contain the German High Seas Fleet within the confines of the North Sea, to support the all-important economic blockade of Germany and to react to any offensive moves the Germans made. The longed-for decisive clash though, didn't materialize. Instead, Jellicoe and his powerful fleet spent months in enforced idleness, waiting for the German fleet to sortie. Despite small initial skirmishes in the Heligoland Bight, and then off the north-eastern English coast near Scarborough, Hartlepool and Yarmouth, the two battlefleets never came to grips. The long-anticipated battle never even occurred when the British entered German waters to attack Cuxhaven, or when the rival battlecruiser forces clashed off Dogger Bank in early 1915. The waiting continued.

The chance for a great victory eventually came in May 1916. Then, Jellicoe put to sea and brought the High Seas Fleet to battle off Jutland. Even then though, that decisive victory eluded Jellicoe, as the Germans managed to extricate themselves from the trap he had laid. Later opportunities were thwarted by German caution, and so the battle of Jutland remained the only major clash of the naval war. Despite the lack of a climactic contest between the two battlefleets, it was the Germans who withdrew back to port, leaving Jellicoe's Grand Fleet in control of the North Sea. This is what turned Jutland into a strategic victory, as it ensured that Britain's blockade of Germany remained in place. Eventually, this more than anything, led to the Germans suing for peace.

In November 1918, the surrender of the German fleet to the Grand Fleet off the Firth of Forth was the dramatic reward for four years of vigilance. There has rarely been a more complete demonstration of the effectiveness of sea power than that ceremony. Sea power, after all, was what the Grand Fleet was all about. By controlling the sea, and thus guaranteeing the effectiveness of the war-winning blockade, the Grand Fleet was the real arbiter of victory in World War I. This book then reveals the composition, organization and effectiveness of Britain's mightiest battlefleet.

The 'Big Cats' at sea, steaming at high speed during a North Sea sweep in 1917. HMS *Tiger* is in the foreground, with HMS *Princess Royal* off her starboard beam. Close off her starboard side is HMS *Lion*, flagship of the Battlecruiser Fleet. From 29 November 1916 until the end of the war, the fleet was under the command of Vice-Admiral William Pakenham.

THE FLEET'S PURPOSE

On 10 February 1906, King Edward VII smashed a bottle of Australian sparkling wine against the bows of the newly christened battleship HMS *Dreadnought*, which then slipped down the stocks and into the cold waters of Portsmouth Harbour. It had taken a few attempts before the wine bottle broke, but eventually the king and several hundred onlookers watched the hull's progress into the water. Also watching the spectacle were representatives of various major naval powers, including one from Imperial Germany. Few of the naval officers watching were in any doubt that their whole world had just been turned on its head. HMS *Dreadnought* was the first of her kind. Until then, battleships usually carried four main guns, in a pair of twin turrets, mounted fore and aft. These battleships lacked an effective means of co-ordinating the fire of these guns, and although these ships were reasonably well protected, they lacked any real speed.

Dreadnought though, was in a league of her own. This warship mounted ten 12in. guns, in twin turrets, which were linked to a fire control system which allowed salvos to be fired with accuracy, even at long range. The new battleship was powered by newly developed steam turbines, which could drive the 21,000-ton warship through the water at 21 knots. Her design had been the result of the logical development in battleship design, but in *Dreadnought* the various design elements had come together to create something truly revolutionary. She was faster, much better armed and as well protected as any other battleship in existence. In essence, *Dreadnought* could out-fight any other warship afloat. By the time *Dreadnought* entered service with the Royal Navy that December, it was clear that this new battleship had rendered all existing capital ships obsolete. As a result, Britain,

HMS *Dreadnought*, the revolutionary battleship which rendered all of her predecessors obsolete and ushered in a new era in naval combat. She was laid down, built, launched, completed and commissioned in just 14 months, between October 1905 and December 1906.

as well as other major naval powers, embarked on a naval arms race, to rebuild their existing fleets in *Dreadnought*'s image.

The new battleship also gave rise to a new name – the 'dreadnought'. These were the battleships built along similar lines, or which represented improvements on the original design. The first of these was laid down in Portsmouth in early December 1906, and four more followed in 1907. By June that year, the first German 'dreadnought' had been laid down, ushering in what amounted to a naval arms race between Britain and Germany. Given the industrial might of Edwardian Britain, it was an unequal contest. By August 1914, the Royal Navy had 20 dreadnoughts in service, with more fitting out, and two more being built for foreign powers commandeered by the British government. In addition, nine battlecruisers were in service – a new design of warship, with more under construction. By contrast, the Imperial German Navy had 13 dreadnoughts and four battlecruisers in service. Britain had won the race, but it came at a price. Setting aside the immense financial cost of this shipbuilding endeavour, this naval escalation also increased tensions between the two countries, and this naval arms race became a contributing factor to the outbreak of the war.

This was ironic, as the building of a powerful dreadnought fleet had originally been seen as a deterrent to war. The Royal Navy had traditionally been in the business of 'sea control' – the global projection of naval power, to secure the seas for British ships and commerce, and to prevent these sea routes being preyed upon by the enemy. In time of war, this also meant denying enemy access to the high seas, thereby bringing economic pressure to bear upon them. This pressure could then be increased by imposing a naval blockade of enemy ports. As the largest naval power in the world, this was all eminently possible for Britain to achieve against virtually any existing power. This global stratagem had been employed by the British since the age of sail, but it took the American naval theorist, Captain Alfred Thayer Mahan, to encapsulate it in the closing years of the 19th century, when he published *The Influence of Sea Power upon History* (1890). Essentially, Mahan extolled the virtues of naval power through a study of the Royal Navy's influence in the rise of British power during the age of sail. This hugely influential work defined the importance of sea power and of naval might.

This study though, had little impact on the British Admiralty, as they had already achieved global control of the seas. Mahan's research, after all, had been

The battlefleet lying at anchor in the main anchorage, during the winter of 1914–15. The viewpoint is from the island of Flotta, looking across Scapa Flow, towards the snow-covered Orphir hills some 7 land miles away to the north-east. In the foreground is the dreadnought HMS *Neptune*.

THE NORTH SEA THEATRE OF OPERATIONS, 1914–18

based on the achievements of the Royal Navy. Still what was important to the Admiralty was retaining their place as the world's premier maritime power. This was widely understood and was the reason why both the British government and the public were willing to support the building of a dreadnought battlefleet. This ensured that Britain would retain its place in the world's naval hierarchy, and so the safety of her maritime trade – the cornerstone of Britain's success - would be assured. This also explains why the sudden expansion of the Imperial German Navy was viewed with suspicion. For the British, their aims were clear – ones based on global sea power. German motives though, were much less obvious. They had no strong naval tradition, and so the building of a dreadnought fleet made little sense to the British.

Before the coming of *Dreadnought*, the Germans had been building a powerful fleet, which would always be smaller than its British counterpart. However, its founder, Admiral von Tirpitz, believed that if concentrated in the North Sea, then it posed a threat to the British, and would force them to match German naval strength in these waters with a similar-sized force of their own. This, Tirpitz felt, would serve to limit Britain's Imperial ambitions, and so give Germany a chance to create overseas colonies of its own. In addition, a German fleet could be deployed in the Baltic Sea, to counter any geopolitical moves made by Russia. In the summer of 1907 though, when work began on the building of four German dreadnoughts, the gauntlet was thrown at Britain's feet. As the coming of *Dreadnought* meant that all existing battleships were obsolete, then Germany, like Britain, had been given a clean slate. Both Admiral von Tirpitz and Kaiser Wilhelm II intended to take full advantage of this.

The creation of Germany's High Seas Fleet had been dismissed as 'the Kaiser's luxury fleet', and this had been tolerated by Britain when its strength consisted

Elements of the 2nd Battle Squadron participating in a North Sea exercise in 1916. In the foreground, HMS *Orion* flies the flag of Rear Admiral Leveson, with HMS *Monarch* and HMS *Thunderer* stationed off her starboard quarter. A fourth dreadnought in the class, HMS *Conqueror*, on the starboard side of the formation, is seen streaming a kite balloon.

of older, conventional 'pre-dreadnought' battleships. However, the building of dreadnoughts meant that Germany's navy now posed a more direct threat to British interests. Another of Mahan's concepts was 'the fleet in being'. Even though it was smaller than the fleet of a larger navy, it still posed a threat by its very existence. As explained before, this forced the larger fleet to deploy a similar-sized force to face it. In the event of a war, the smaller fleet had no chance of defeating the larger one, but it could threaten its control of the seas. Despite the loss of the smaller fleet in battle, it could still gravely weaken the larger fleet – another small fleet could join the conflict and defeat the weakened naval superpower. This was the policy of *Risikogedanke* ('Risk Theory') developed by von Tirpitz, which in theory reduced the risk of a naval war with Britain by making it too costly an option for the British to contemplate.

This policy, set against a backdrop of European treaties and alliances, meant that, potentially, the Royal Navy could be markedly weakened in a naval war with Germany. This in turn would allow another smaller navy – for instance the French *Marine Nationale* – to take on the British and wrest control of the sea from them. Mahan's proposed stratagem, however, was unlikely to take place as it relied on a second sizeable maritime power – France, Russia, the United States or even Japan – allying themselves with Imperial Germany. In the end, only the very minor naval power of Austria-Hungary formed a pact with Germany. As those forces were restricted to the Adriatic Sea, they were incapable of causing sleepless nights in the British Admiralty.

At the outbreak of war, it became clear to the Germans that the Risk Theory wasn't going to work. So, it was replaced by another stratagem, *Kräfteausgleich* ('Force Balancing'). Essentially, this meant that the High Seas Fleet would attempt to 'nibble away' at the Grand Fleet, ambushing and sinking parts of the British fleet, until the two sides reached parity in numbers. Then, the Germans would seek a decisive battle, ideally also on advantageous terms, which would result in the destruction of the Grand Fleet. The British antidote to either the Risk Theory or Force Balancing stratagems was simply to outbuild their opponents. Not only was this an unanswerable policy, but it also significantly reduced the offensive options of the Germans, as it was likely that the British would be able to outnumber and outgun their opponents in any naval clash of arms.

In January 1915, when the two sides clashed at Dogger Bank, the British had 24 dreadnoughts in service and ten battlecruisers, against the German total of 16 dreadnoughts and five battlecruisers, one of which was cornered in Turkish waters. This disparity only increased as the war went on. By 1918, the Germans had 19 dreadnoughts and five battlecruisers available (discounting the *Goeben* in Turkish service), to the Royal Navy's 34 dreadnoughts and 'fast battleships' and 12 battlecruisers. The odds lengthened even more after a US Navy squadron of four dreadnoughts joined the Grand Fleet. Another battlecruiser, *Furious*, was converted into an aircraft carrier in 1917–18, joining another prototype carrier, *Argus*, which became part of the fleet weeks before the end of the war. Effectively, the

British policy of building enough dreadnoughts to ensure that their fleet couldn't be defeated proved highly effective.

Since 1908, the British Admiralty had adopted a rule of thumb that the Royal Navy would be 60 per cent larger than the German fleet – a policy which was agreed by the British Government in early 1912. This in turn led to the building of a new naval dockyard at Rosyth in Scotland and the expansion of other shipbuilding facilities. Consequently, from well before the outbreak of war, the British policy of outbuilding its most likely enemy was firmly established and the favourable naval balance between the two rivals studiously maintained. Of course, not every capital ship available to the British Admiralty was deployed with the Grand Fleet. While almost all of them were, occasionally some would be deployed elsewhere or were detached to serve in the Mediterranean Fleet. However, the vast majority of these capital ships were concentrated in the Grand Fleet, ready to counter any move the enemy might make.

The destroyer HMS *Broke* was built in Cowes for the Chilean Navy but was purchased by the Admiralty when the war began, becoming a Faulknor-class flotilla leader. At Jutland, she formed part of the 4th Destroyer Flotilla, and in a night-time encounter she launched a torpedo which may well have struck the light cruiser *Elbing*. Commander Allen's destroyer was undamaged, but in a second clash with the dreadnought *Westfalen* was badly damaged, with more than 50 of her crew killed.

While many politicians and senior naval officers might have hoped for a decisive clash soon after the war began, Admiral Jellicoe and others adopted a more realistic view, based on this disparity in numbers. As the German fleet was smaller, the likelihood was that in the event of a naval clash, it would break off the action before the British could use their greater numbers to overwhelm their opponents. Jellicoe still sought just such a decisive clash, but for him, it was just as important to preserve his fleet to maintain this numerical advantage. Essentially, his aim was to avoid defeat, rather than to risk part of his fleet in the pursuit of victory. After all, his fleet's main task was to prevent the Germans from breaking the economic blockade, which would eventually bring Germany to its knees.

Other more conventional aims, such as the protection of the British coast or even the destruction of the enemy battlefleet, were considered secondary to the maintenance of the blockade and ensuring the Grand Fleet remained the dominant naval force in the North Sea. There was little glory in this approach, as there was scant chance of a Trafalgar-style victory which could end the naval war at a stroke. Nevertheless, Jellicoe almost achieved that at Jutland. Afterwards, he was criticized for his cautiousness, and his inability to strike a decisive blow against the enemy. This though, misses the point of the Grand Fleet. In terms of the long-term goals of the containment of the enemy fleet and the continuance of the blockade, Jellicoe and his Grand Fleet were doing exactly what was required. These two aims were all it took to ensure an Allied victory. This was a new, very modern kind of war. It wouldn't be won by crushing the enemy fleet. Instead, it would be the application of sea power alone which would achieve a decisive victory in the naval war. It was a stratagem which would have made Alfred Thayer Mahan proud.

FLEET FIGHTING POWER

THE SHIPS

At the heart of the Grand Fleet was the battlefleet of dreadnought battleships. While the coming of *Dreadnought* had angered some, as it rendered Britain's existing battlefleet obsolete, the development was irrevocable. If the Admiralty didn't embrace the 'dreadnought age', then other naval rivals would. So, supported by both the British government and the public, the Admiralty embarked on a rebuilding of its battlefleet along the lines of *Dreadnought*. Their design was dominated by their main guns. *Dreadnought* and her immediate Bellerophon-class successors mounted 12in. Mk X guns, while the three St Vincent-class ships that followed, along with *Neptune* and *Colossus*, mounted a slightly modified 12in. Mk XI gun, which had marginally better hitting power. What let the early dreadnoughts down, though, was their gun layout.

The three Bellerophons and three St Vincents adopted a similar gun configuration as *Dreadnought*, where only eight guns could fire together in a broadside. Due to the layout, one twin turret was blocked by the superstructure, so couldn't add its weight to the salvo. *Neptune* and *Colossus* attempted to overcome this by allowing their two midships turrets to fire on either beam, through a gap in the superstructure. In practice, though, blast damage made this impractical, so they too could only fire four of their five turrets. Still, the Admiralty viewed the design of their dreadnoughts as an evolutionary process. This was summed up by the

The Colossus-class dreadnought HMS Hercules *formed part of the 1st Battle Squadron at Jutland, but after the battle she was transferred to the 4th Battle Squadron and became the flagship of Vice-Admiral Doveton Sturdee, the victor of the battle of the Falklands (1914). A vice-admiral's flag can be seen flying from the top of the foremast.*

popular slogan, 'Build first and build fast, each one better than the last'.

In 1909 plans were developed for a larger dreadnought, or 'super dreadnought', mounting more powerful 13.5in. Mk V guns. Their designer's solution to the gun layout problem was the adoption of 'superfiring' turrets. One of them was mounted behind the other, but was raised up so it could fire over the top of the first turret. So, in the Orion-class 'super dreadnoughts', the two forward and two after turrets were mounted in this way, while the fifth midships turret was given a clear field of fire to either beam. All ten guns could thus fire on the same broadside. Four of these Orions were built. Not only did they have a sensible gun layout, but the guns themselves had both an improved range and a greater hitting power. They were also backed up by a better fire control system.

The Queen Elizabeth-class fast battleship HMS *Barham*, pictured from a passing airship in 1918. She mounted eight 15in. guns in four turrets. At Jutland, *Barham* was the flagship of the 5th Battle Squadron, flying the flag of Rear Admiral Hugh Evan-Thomas.

The next batch were the five 'super dreadnoughts' of the Iron Duke class. These were slightly larger than the Orions, which allowed the designers to improve the layout of the ship and provide a larger secondary gun armament. These ships marked the end of the line for this type of dreadnought. In 1912, concerns about the reports that maritime rivals were building ships mounting 14in. guns led to a rethink of the dreadnought design. The next class was intended to be an improved version of the Iron Dukes, but the Admiralty's insistence on the mounting of 15in. guns caused a major change of design. The result was the 'fast battleship', a kind of 'extra super dreadnought', built to carry eight of these larger and more powerful guns, in four twin turrets, arranged in a superfiring arrangement at the battleship's bow and stern.

When the first of these, *Queen Elizabeth,* entered service in January 1915, she represented a culmination of the dreadnought design – a battleship so valuable that despite the mass scrapping of the fleet as a result of post-war disarmament treaties, these 15in. 'fast battleships' were retained and became the core of the post-war fleet. The five battleships of the class were quickly followed by five more, this time of the Royal Sovereign class, which were similar but built to a less exacting standard. During the battle of Jutland, these 15in. battleships made an extremely favourable impression and marked the way forward in battleship design, not just for Britain but for other maritime powers too.

The battlefleet also included three dreadnoughts which were being built in British shipyards for other navies when the war began. Two Turkish dreadnoughts were seized in August 1914, and duly became the *Agincourt* (mounting 14 12in. guns) and the *Erin* (with ten 13½in. guns). A third dreadnought being built for the Chilean Navy was also under construction and she was duly purchased

13

and became the *Canada*, mounting ten 14in. guns. The result of all this was a dreadnought battlefleet which, at Jutland, was made up of 22 dreadnoughts of various classes, and six 15in. battleships. Just as importantly, extensive training had by then welded these battleships into a formidable naval weapon.

While it was extremely difficult to deploy this number of ships into a battle formation, this was achieved at Jutland with an impressive degree of precision, despite the poor visibility due to funnel smoke and mist. In theory, the firepower deployed – a collective broadside of a little over 145 tons of armour-piercing shells – was truly devastating, especially as these guns had a range of more than 10 miles. However, making sure the battlefleet was deployed in a way that made the most of this firepower was a monumental challenge for any fleet commander, including Admiral Jellicoe. It was potentially a truly lethal naval weapon – and one which, when deployed together, was capable of annihilating its German opponents. Never before or since would such a powerful collection of battleships be concentrated into one single battlefleet.

While both the British and the Germans made limited use of older 'pre-dreadnought' battleships, both sides realized these would be no match for the enemy in a naval clash. Each navy though, used these older ships differently. The British relegated them to secondary roles, such as coastal defence, or to deploy them in the Mediterranean, where there was little to threaten them. By contrast the Germans concentrated theirs into a battle squadron, which was attached to their battlefleet. In other words, they used them to partially offset their numerical inferiority. This, of course, placed these vulnerable capital ships in harm's way. At Jutland though, they were tucked at the back of the battlefleet, and played little part in the battle.

The 'eyes and ears' of any fleet of this period were its cruisers. The Royal Navy was well provided with them, with just over 120 of them in commission at the start of the war. Half of these were newly built, less than seven years old. However, only a third of these cruisers were deployed with the Grand Fleet. The remainder were stationed elsewhere, protecting the world's sea lanes, and hunting down a dwindling number of their German counterparts. The cruiser itself was a long-established type of warship, designed primarily for trade protection and scouting. By the last decade of the previous century these had evolved along two main lines – the light cruiser and the armoured cruiser. The first group were the more numerous, replacing the older form of 'protected cruiser' which were partially armoured, with a new breed where the emphasis was on speed rather than protection.

These light cruisers included a group which were sometimes known as 'scout cruisers', although reconnaissance ahead of the battlefleet was really the main job of all these British light cruisers. Although numerous classes were built, and each succeeding class tended to be larger than their predecessors, they almost all shared a similar general design. British light cruisers had narrow, sleek hulls topped by four funnels, while their guns were arrayed at along each beam, with more at the bow and stern. This armament was augmented by torpedo tubes. They could make something in the region of 25–30 knots, which gave them a useful edge of speed over most larger cruisers or capital ships. Their secondary purpose when serving with the battlefleet was to protect the capital ships from attacks by enemy torpedo boats or destroyers. They were able to form a shield, positioning themselves between the likely enemy avenue of attack and their target. This made these vessels very useful components of the fleet.

Also included in the Grand Fleet were squadrons of older armoured cruisers. In the 1890s, 'protected cruisers' – those with some armour protecting their decks, machinery and magazines – grew in size, so designers went a step further. The result was the armoured cruiser: larger ships with more powerful engines, larger guns, and thicker and more extensive armour. By the first years of the 20th century, these warships were protected by armoured belts up to 6in. thick, and some mounted main batteries of 9.2in. guns. This, combined with their speed of around 23 knots, made them powerful warships, albeit ones which couldn't take on dreadnoughts or even pre-dreadnought battleships. This was their real flaw. They were primarily designed to hunt down enemy raiders on the high seas. Inevitably though, when attached to the Grand Fleet, the danger was that they would be drawn into a fight with far more powerful opponents. This is exactly what happened at Jutland, when three of them were lost.

The most spectacular naval development to spring from the creation of *Dreadnought* was the 'battlecruiser'. The first was laid down in 1906, and despite their evident shortcomings they continued to be built as late as 1920. They were, as the name suggests, an amalgam of the dreadnought battleship and the cruiser. As such, they combined the firepower of a dreadnought with the greater speed of the faster cruisers. Warship design during this period though, was essentially the balancing of three factors – firepower, protection and speed. Any emphasis on one or two of these meant the consequent reduction of the third factor. So it was with battlecruisers, where protection was sacrificed in order to emphasize firepower and speed.

The Royal Sovereign-class (or Revenge-class) fast battleship HMS *Ramillies*, pictured at anchor in Scapa Flow in late 1917. Unusually, the 15in.-gun dreadnought is painted in a dazzle camouflage scheme, made up of dark blue, dark grey, mid-grey and black stripes, in places with white edging, over a base of light pink forward, mid-grey aft and light olive green amidships.

The original role of these battlecruisers was to hunt down and sink enemy cruisers, including armoured ones. In the battle of the Falkland Islands in 1914, this is exactly what two of them did. This use of *Invincible* and *Inflexible* was just what these ships were designed for. These two battlecruisers, and their sister ship *Indomitable,* were built between 1906 and 1909, and were followed by three more, the last of which, *Australia*, entered service in 1913. Each of these battlecruisers mounted eight 12in. guns, but the next four, the 'Splendid Cats' as they were called, carried the 13½in. guns mounted in 'super dreadnoughts'. The design was flawed though, as the size of their guns was out of proportion to the weakness of their armour. Initially, battlecruisers were used to hunt down German warships which were at large overseas, such as von Spee's squadron which was destroyed off the Falklands. Inevitably though, due to their impressive firepower, these battlecruisers were attached to the Grand Fleet.

Here their role in any naval clash was less clear. They had performed well at the battle of Heligoland Bight in 1914, as their opponents were mere cruisers. The British battlecruisers also did well at the battle of Dogger Bank the following January, when they engaged their outnumbered German counterparts, sinking a German armoured cruiser, *Blücher*. They had the speed to range ahead of the battlefleet and the firepower to take on the German scouting groups, made up of battlecruisers and cruisers. Inevitably, however, like the older armoured cruisers, it was almost impossible to avoid them being drawn into a major engagement. This became even more likely when they were concentrated into their own Battlecruiser Fleet, whose main job was to locate the enemy and draw them towards the main British battlefleet. This placed them very much in harm's way.

What naval commanders didn't account for was the vulnerability of these battlecruisers to enemy fire. This should have been readily apparent – they were, after all, provided with the armour only to protect them against the largest guns carried by enemy armoured cruisers. When engaged by their German counterparts, armed with 11in. and 12in. guns, then their vulnerability was exposed. This led to the loss of three British battlecruisers at Jutland: *Invincible*, *Indefatigable* and *Queen Mary*. Afterwards, the risk to the remaining battlecruisers was reduced by introducing improved ammunition-handling procedures, and the battlecruisers still under construction were provided with more armour. These though, did nothing to deal with the fundamental problem that these battlecruisers weren't built for a fight with equally well-armed opponents.

The remaining significant element of the Grand Fleet was its destroyer force. The development of the self-propelled torpedo in 1866 altered the face of naval warfare. It took time to perfect their design, but by the 1880s the leading maritime powers began building flotillas of small torpedo-armed warships. Although small and limited in their range, these torpedo boats could

The dreadnought HMS *Orion*, namesake of her class, pictured while part of the Grand Fleet which accepted the surrender of the High Seas Fleet on 21 November 1918. By this stage she mounted a Sopwith Pup biplane on a flying-off platform atop 'B' turret.

THE GRAND FLEET (ADM JELLICOE) AUGUST 1914

Iron Duke (fleet flagship)

attached: *Sappho* (protected cruiser) & *Oak* (destroyer)

1st Battle Sqn (V Adm Bayly, R Adm Evan-Thomas)

Marlborough (flagship), *Colossus, Hercules, Neptune*
St Vincent (rear flag), *Collingwood, Vanguard, Superb*
attached: *Bellona* (light cruiser) & *Cyclops* (repair ship)

2nd Battle Sqn (V Adm Warrender)

King George V (flagship), *Ajax, Audacious, Centurion*
Orion (flagship, R Adm Arburthnot), *Conqueror, Monarch, Thunderer*
attached: *Boadicea* (light cruiser) & *Assistance* (repair ship)

3rd Battle Sqn (V Adm Bradford)

King Edward VII (flagship), *Commonwealth, Zealandia, Dominion*
Hibernia (flagship, R Adm Browning), *Africa, Britannia, Hindustan*

4th Battle Sqn (V Adm Gamble)

Dreadnought (flagship), *Temeraire, Bellerophon*
attached: *Blonde* (light cruiser)

1st Battlecruiser Sqn (V Adm Beatty)

Lion (flagship), *Princess Royal, Queen Mary, New Zealand*

2nd Cruiser Sqn (R Adm Gough-Calthorpe)

Shannon (flagship), *Achilles, Cochrane, Natal*

3rd Cruiser Sqn (R Adm Pakenham)

Antrim (flagship), *Argyll, Devonshire, Roxburgh*

1st Light Cruiser Sqn (Cmdre Goodenough)

Southampton (flagship), *Birmingham, Lowestoft, Nottingham.*

2nd Destroyer Flotilla (Capt Hawkesley)

flotilla leader: *Active* (scout cruiser), plus 20 H-class destroyers: *Acorn, Alarm, Brisk, Cameleon, Comet, Fury, Goldfinch, Hope, Larne, Lyra, Martin, Minstrel, Nemesis, Nereide, Nymphe, Redpole, Rifleman, Ruby, Sheldrake, Staunch*

4th Destroyer Flotilla (Capt Wintour)

flotilla leader: *Swift* (destroyer leader), plus 20 K-class destroyers: *Acasta, Achates, Ambuscade, Ardent, Christopher, Cockatrice, Contest, Fortune, Garland, Hardy, Lynx, Midge, Owl, Paragon, Porpoise, Shark, Sparrowhawk, Spitfire, Unity, Victor*

Minesweeping Flotilla (Cdr Preston)

flotilla leader: *Skipjack*, plus *Gossamer, Speedwell* (Sharpshooter-class torpedo gunboats), *Circe, Leda* (Alarm-class torpedo gunboats)

potentially launch massed torpedo attacks against an enemy battlefleet. The antidote was to provide larger warships with small, quick-firing guns for 'anti-torpedo' defence. Flotillas of other small, fast boats were then designed, armed with the same quick-firing anti-torpedo weapons. Their job was to head off any torpedo boat attack and sink the enemy before they reached the battlefleet.

These new little warships were dubbed 'torpedo-boat destroyers', a title which was soon abbreviated to 'destroyers'. Inevitably, by the early 20th century, these became larger and mounted torpedoes themselves. This gave them a dual offensive and defensive role. By 1914, two destroyer flotillas were attached to the Grand Fleet, each made up of 20 destroyers, plus a flotilla leader – either a scout cruiser or a larger 'destroyer leader'. Each flotilla was made up of a single class of destroyers, built between 1910 and 1913, and armed with two or three 4in. guns and two torpedo tubes. These destroyers were capable of making 27–30 knots – fast enough to head off their enemy counterparts and deal with them. For the most part, these destroyers were larger and slightly more seaworthy than the torpedo boats favoured by the Germans.

THE GRAND FLEET (ADM JELLICOE) 31 MAY 1916 (BATTLE OF JUTLAND)

Iron Duke (fleet flagship)
attached: *Oak* (destroyer)

THE BATTLEFLEET

2nd Battle Sqn (V Adm Jerram)

King George V (flagship), *Ajax*, *Centurion*, *Erin* (1st Division)

Orion (flagship, R Adm Leveson), *Monarch*, *Conqueror*, *Thunderer* (2nd Division)

4th Battle Sqn (V Adm Doveton Sturdee)

Iron Duke (fleet flagship), *Royal Oak*, *Superb* (flagship, R Adm Duff), *Canada* (3rd Division)

Benbow (flagship), *Bellerophon*, *Temeraire*, *Vanguard* (4th Division)

1st Battle Sqn (V Adm Burney)

Colossus (flagship, R Adm Gaunt), *Collingwood*, *Neptune*, *St Vincent* (5th Division)

Marlborough (flagship), *Revenge*, *Hercules*, *Agincourt* (6th Division)

3rd Battlecruiser Sqn (R Adm Hood) – temporarily attached to battlefleet

Invincible (flagship), *Inflexible*, *Indomitable*

1st Cruiser Sqn (R Adm Arbuthnot)

Defence (flagship), *Warrior*, *Duke of Edinburgh*, *Black Prince*

2nd Cruiser Sqn (R Adm Heath)

Minotaur (flagship), *Hampshire*, *Cochrane*, *Shannon*

4th Light Cruiser Sqn (Cmdre Le Mesurier)

Calliope (flagship), *Constance*, *Caroline*, *Royalist*, *Comus*

attached light cruisers: *Active*, *Bellone*, *Blanche*, *Boadicea*, *Canterbury*, *Dover*

other attached vessels: *Abdiel* (minelayer)

4th Destroyer Flotilla (Capt Wintour)

flotilla leader: *Tipperary* (destroyer leader), plus 18 K-class destroyers: *Acasta*, *Achates*, *Ambuscade*, *Ardent*, *Broke*, *Christopher*, *Contest*, *Fortune*, *Garland*, *Hardy*, *Midge*, *Ophelia*, *Owl*, *Porpoise*, *Shark*, *Sparrowhawk*, *Spitfire*, *Unity*

11th Destroyer Flotilla (Cmdre Hawksley)

flotilla leader: *Castor* (light cruiser), plus 15 M-class destroyers: *Kempenfelt*, *Magic*, *Mandate*, *Manners*, *Marne*, *Martial*, *Michael*, *Milbrook*, *Minion*, *Mons*, *Moon*, *Morning Star*, *Mounsey*, *Mystic*, *Ossory*

12th Destroyer Flotilla (Capt Stirling)

flotilla leader: *Faulknor* (destroyer leader), plus 15 M-class destroyers: *Maenad*, *Marksman*, *Marvel*, *Mary Rose*, *Menace*, *Mindful*, *Mischief*, *Munster*, *Narwhal*, *Nessus*, *Noble*, *Nonsuch*, *Obedient*, *Onslaught*, *Opal*.

BATTLECRUISER FLEET (V ADM BEATTY)

1st Battlecruiser Sqn (V Adm Beatty): *Lion* (flagship), *Princess Royal*, *Queen Mary*, *Tiger*

2nd Battlecruiser Sqn (R Adm Packenham)

New Zealand (flagship), *Indefatigable*

5th Battle Sqn (R Adm Evan-Thomas) – temporarily attached to Battlecruiser Fleet

Barham (flagship), *Valiant*, *Warspite*, *Malaya*

1st Light Cruiser Sqn (Cmdre Alexander-Sinclair)

Galatea (flagship), *Phaeton*, *Inconstant*, *Cordelia*

2nd Light Cruiser Sqn (Cmdre Goodenough)

Southampton (flagship), *Birmingham*, *Nottingham*, *Dublin*

2nd Light Cruiser Sqn (R Adm Napier)

Falmouth (flagship), *Yarmouth*, *Birkenhead*, *Gloucester*

1st Destroyer Flotilla (Capt Roper)

flotilla leader: *Fearless* (light cruiser), plus nine A-class destroyers: *Acheron*, *Ariel*, *Attack*, *Badger*, *Defender*, *Goshawk*, *Hydra*, *Lapwing*, *Lizard*

9th/10th Destroyer Flotillas (combined) (Cdr Goldsmith)

flotilla leader: *Lydiard* (destroyer leader), plus seven M-class destroyers: *Landrail*, *Laurel*, *Liberty*, *Moorsom*, *Morris*, *Termagant*, *Turbulent*

13th Destroyer Flotilla (Capt Farie)

flotilla leader: *Champion* (light cruiser), plus ten M-class destroyers: *Morseby*, *Narborough*, *Nerissa*, *Nestor*, *Nicator*, *Nomad*, *Obdurate*, *Onslow*, *Pelican*, *Petard*

attached vessel: *Engadine* (seaplane carrier)

The challenge facing the Commander-in-Chief of the Grand Fleet was to weld these disparate elements into an effective fighting force. Each element – the dreadnought battleships of the battlefleet, the cruiser squadrons and the destroyer flotillas – all had a clear operational role. To some extent, so too did the fleet's battlecruisers, although their design made them poorly suited to fighting equally well-armed capital ships. A clash of battlecruisers at the time was likened to firing shotguns at cardboard boxes – an analogy which had some merit. The variety of vessels also imposed limitations on their use. For instance, the battlefleet was slower than the other elements of the fleet, and so the fleet commander had to rely on his scouting forces to guide it into contact with the enemy. Similarly, destroyers had a limited range, which in turn limited the radius of action of the Grand Fleet if it was to operate as a fully effective combined force.

TECHNICAL FACTORS
Guns

Dreadnought was the first true 'big-gun battleship' with a main battery of a single calibre. The secondary battery was seen as of no real use, other than as anti-torpedo boat defence. Later though, it was felt that these dreadnoughts needed a more effective defence against enemy destroyers, so her successor class was equipped with a secondary battery of 4in. guns. By the time the Iron Duke class was designed, these were increased to 6in. guns, a weapon which was also mounted in *Agincourt, Canada, Erin* and the two classes of 15in. gun 'fast battleships'. The main battery, though, remained the *raison d'être* for these dreadnoughts, supported by a modern fire control system which allowed these guns to be fired accurately at a range of up to 12 miles.

The main guns mounted in the capital ships of the battlefleet and the Battlecruiser Fleet were as follows:

12in. (30.5cm)/45cal Mk X	Dreadnought, Bellerophon, Agincourt, Invincible and Indefatigable classes
12in. (30.5cm)/50cal Mk XI	St Vincent, Neptune and Colossus classes
13½in. (34.3cm)/45cal Mk V	Orion, King George V, Iron Duke, Erin, Lion, Queen Mary and Tiger classes
14in. (35.6cm)/45cal Mk I	Canada class
15in. (38.1cm)/42cal Mk I	Queen Elizabeth, Royal Sovereign, Renown, Courageous and Hood classes
18in. (45.7cm)/40cal Mk I	Furious class

Not all of these saw active service with the Grand Fleet. The light battlecruiser *Furious*, the only ship of her class, was uniquely armed with two single 18in. turrets. However, while nearing completion her forward one was removed and replaced by a flight deck. Although *Furious* joined the Grand Fleet in July 1917, this hybrid carrier-battlecruiser conducted sea trials to evaluate her performance as a makeshift aircraft carrier. That November she returned to the shipyard to have her remaining turret removed, and the flight deck was extended to cover the after part of the ship. The battlecruiser *Hood*, laid down in 1916, wasn't completed until after the war, by which time her three sister ships were scrapped while still on the stocks, and the Grand Fleet had been dissolved.

The two types of 12in. guns had a maximum range of around 20,000yds (18,290m), with an armour penetration of around 8–9in. In theory, these guns had a rate of fire of around one salvo every 40 seconds. The charge of an armour-piercing shell weighed around 27lb (12.4kg). As the gun size increased, so too did the size and penetrative ability of the shell. The 13.5in. Mk V gun introduced in 1912 had a slightly greater range (23,740yds/21,710m) at 20° elevation, with a bursting charge of 40lb (18.1kg) of Lyddite and an armour penetration of 10.6in. While this wasn't able to penetrate the thickest belt armour of a German dreadnought, it could cause extensive damage elsewhere, especially at long range, when the shell trajectory was more vertical than horizontal.

The 15in. Mk I gun was in a league of its own, firing an armour-piercing shell with a 60½lb (27.4kg) Lyddite charge, at a range of 25,000yds (22,860m) at a gun elevation of 22.5°. This had a strike velocity of 1,317ft per second and was capable of penetrating 13.4in. of enemy armour. What all this meant was that in theory, when working together, the battlefleet could engage an enemy at a range of up to 10 nautical miles with a fair chance of inflicting serious damage upon any target, including a dreadnought. Of course, naval gunnery wasn't just a matter of pointing the guns at the enemy and opening fire. During World War I, naval gunnery was a complicated science, where gunnery direction systems were used to make sure that these shells could hit their target.

This procedure began with the visual tracking of the enemy using Barr & Stroud coincidence rangefinders. An operator would use this to determine the range and bearing of the enemy. This information was then passed on to the fire control team, located deep inside the firing ship. There, the information would be entered into a Dreyer Fire Control Table, together with other information on angles of deflection, target and firer's speed, weather and temperature. It would then mechanically calculate a firing solution, which was modified by spotters, who watched the fall of shot of previous salvos and fed in corrections – whether the shots were on target, over or under. The result, which was then passed on to the gun

While under way, the boiler room of a dreadnought battleship was something of an inferno, filled with noise, heat and choking coal dust. The reliance of dreadnoughts on coal ended with the switch to fuel oil, used by the fast battleships of the Queen Elizabeth class. This though, meant the importation of oil, rather than the use of home-produced high-grade anthracite coal.

turrets by the gunnery officer, told the gun crews the bearing and elevation at which they should fire. The calculations took seconds to complete, but accuracy depended on the steady flow of accurate information, and so communications within the ship were key.

This calculation also considered the location of the turrets. On a typical dreadnought of the Grand Fleet, these could be 400ft apart. So, for the shells all to land in the same area, each turret had slightly different firing solutions, as the results were first passed through a convergence corrector. Then, inside the turret, the gunlayer would read the required elevation on a receiver, while the turret trainer would do the same. Once the guns were aimed correctly, the turret officer would flip a switch, which lit a 'ready' lamp in the Gunnery Director position. There, once all turrets were ready, the ship's gunnery officer would give the order 'Shoot!', his gunlayer would pull an electronic trigger and all of the dreadnought's turrets would open fire in a co-ordinated salvo.

This central control could be overridden for safety's sake, but usually this centrally controlled method was the one which was used. Once the guns had fired, they were reloaded using automated shell hoists and hydraulic rammers. Of course, the flight time of the shells depended on the range. At Jutland, when the British battlefleet first opened fire on its German counterparts, the two fleets were approximately 12,000–14,000yds apart. At that range, the flight time would be approximately 20 seconds. The fall of shot would be observed closely by a spotting team, who would feed the information into the system, which was already calculating the information required to fire the next salvo.

A well-trained crew in a dreadnought could fire a salvo every 40–50 seconds. While the guns had a much greater theoretical range, accuracy depended on the ability of the gunnery teams to see the target and the capacity of the guns to elevate, which in turn limited a dreadnought's effective range to approximately 12 miles. Battle range though, was usually half of that, to ensure a clear view of the target amid all the funnel smoke and shell splashes generated in a fleet engagement.

Armour and Propulsion

While a dreadnought was essentially an immensely powerful mobile gun battery, its effectiveness as a fighting unit depended heavily on three other factors – its ability to manoeuvre, the degree of protection it had to absorb enemy hits and the efficiency of its damage control systems to cope with debilitating hits, which might degrade the ship's ability to move and fight. From *Dreadnought* on, all modern battleships in the Grand Fleet were powered by modern steam turbines, which generated considerably more power than earlier marine propulsion plants. In *Dreadnought* and her immediate successors, four Parsons turbines were powered by high-pressure steam produced in 18 Babcock & Wilcox boilers. These generated 23,000 steam horsepower (shp), which, when directed to the vessel's two massive propellers and shafts, could generate speeds of more than 20 knots.

The 13½in. guns of the dreadnought HMS *King George V*, trained to starboard during a gunnery exercise in the North Sea during the winter of 1917–18. In the foreground is 'Q' turret, mounted amidships, while further aft, behind the after superstructure, are the guns of the superfiring 'X' turret, and then 'Y' turret further aft and beneath them.

These vulnerable machinery spaces needed to be protected, as did the ship's magazines, and so armoured belts were created, girding the hull of the capital ship. In *Dreadnought*, these varied in thickness, with the greatest thickness around these key areas, and the belt tapering off towards the two ends. In *Dreadnought*, her belt varied from 4in. to 11in. in thickness, while her turret faces, the barbettes which protected the inner workings of the turret mounts, and the ship's conning tower were all protected by 11in. of hardened steel. *Dreadnought* was less well protected against long-range plunging fire though, but her decks were still plated with armour ranging from 1.5 to 3in. in thickness. In addition, armoured bulkheads provided lateral internal protection within the ship. Armoured protection was marginally increased in later dreadnoughts, with the Queen Elizabeth class fitted with a belt up to 14in. thick.

This additional weight was absorbed by a more efficient propulsion system, which generated 56,000shp, giving the class a maximum speed of 23 knots. This was achieved by fitting more advanced engines, more boilers, and significantly, changing the fuel. The Queen Elizabeth class were the first purely oil-fired capital ships in the fleet. At the time this was a radical departure from the traditional coal-fired system, but it was one that offered significant advantages. As well as being far more efficient and giving the ships a greater radius of action without refuelling, they performed better too. Oil-powered capital ships enjoyed a faster acceleration than coal-powered ones, they could maintain high speeds for longer, and they were easier to refuel. An additional benefit was that their funnels didn't emit thick black smoke, which could betray the presence of a coal-fired warship long before the vessel itself could be seen over the horizon.

Emerging Technologies

Mines had been a factor in naval warfare since the mid-19th century, and their effectiveness had grown considerably during the interim. By 1914, there were two main types: controlled mines, which were used defensively and activated from the shore, and independent mines, deployed at sea, which could be tethered or mobile. Controlled minefields were laid around Scapa Flow, and were activated electrically when an enemy vessel was spotted entering the mined area. In October 1918, the controlled minefield in Hoxa Sound, the main entrance to the anchorage, was activated, destroying a U-boat, UB-116, which was attempting to sneak into Scapa Flow.

Independent mines took several forms, the most common used by the Germans being a 'Carbonit' contact mine. Once laid, it was tethered to a sinker on the seabed, and a buoyancy chamber allowed the mine to rise to a pre-selected depth, guided by a hydrostat. It was detonated when the horns on the casing encountered a passing ship. Various modifications existed, including the antenna mine, where a wire antenna did the same job as the horns, while other mines floated at a pre-set depth, using an automatic depth-setting device. The Germans laid fields off Britain's North Sea coast, while the British made extensive use of mines too, laying the Northern Barrage between Orkney and Norway, as well as across the Dover Straits.

These mines, obviously, were a limiting factor in naval operations around the North Sea, and caused losses to the Grand Fleet. The most significant of these came in August 1914, when the King George V-class dreadnought *Audacious* sank after being mined off the coast of Donegal. Even more notable, on the evening of 5 June 1916, the armoured cruiser HMS *Hampshire* struck a mine off the west coast of Orkney and sank with the loss of almost all of her crew. Aboard the *Hampshire*, and lost in the disaster, was Field Marshal Lord Kitchener, who was then Britain's Secretary of State for War. At the time he was on his way to Russia, to meet his Russian counterparts.

Another relatively new development in naval warfare was the self-propelled torpedo. First developed in the 1860s, by 1914 it had become a reliable and deadly weapon. Although torpedoes were carried by a range of surface ships, including capital ships, they were mainly mounted in destroyers and torpedo boats. British 21in. (53.3cm) torpedoes of this period had a range of up to 5,500yds, speeds of 30–35 knots and carried a warhead of over 500lb (230kg) of TNT. German torpedoes were of a similar design, but the Imperial German Navy favoured a 50cm (19.7in.) version, the G/6, which had a smaller warhead of 164kg (362lb).

The real torpedo threat to the Grand Fleet was posed by U-boats rather than torpedo boats. In the first year of war alone, the Royal Navy lost a pre-dreadnought battleship (*Formidable*), a seaplane carrier (*Hermes*) and six cruisers

On 2 August 1917, Squadron Leader Edwin Dunning made the first deck landing on an aircraft carrier under way. The hybrid battlecruiser carrier, HMS *Furious*, was steaming in Scapa Flow at the time, and Dunning's Sopwith Pup was grabbed by the deck crew before it rolled over the side of the deck. Five days later, Dunning repeated the feat, but later that day he died when, on a third landing, the deck crew were unable to grab the fighter before it plunged over the side into the sea.

(*Aboukir*, *Birmingham*, *Cressy*, *Hawke*, *Hogue* and *Pathfinder*) to U-boats. As a result, extensive anti-torpedo precautions were taken when the Grand Fleet was in Scapa Flow, and regular anti-submarine sweeps were conducted in the North Sea. Nevertheless, U-boats remained a serious threat to the Grand Fleet throughout the war.

The other major technological development, apart from the wireless – which will be examined later – was naval aviation. The German Naval Airship Division was responsible for conducting Zeppelin reconnaissance flights over the North Sea, from bases near Germany's North Sea coast. The Germans also commissioned eight Schütte-Laz wooden-framed airships and six more experimental types, but it was the metal-framed Zeppelin which proved the most effective. In all, 59 of these were commissioned, and from 1915 on, as well as naval reconnaissance, they were used in bombing raids over Britain – with a total of 5,751 bombs being dropped by them during the war. London alone was raided 12 times. With a maximum speed of over 64mph, they proved difficult to intercept, but a number were lost to ground fire or through accidental damage.

The Royal Navy had its own airship programme, and these were eventually used in the latter years of the war to protect convoys and to conduct anti U-boat sweeps. However, seaplanes were also used, designed to operate from seaplane carriers. In 1914, HMS *Ark Royal* became the first vessel designed and built exclusively as a seaplane carrier. On Christmas Day 1914, three Royal Navy seaplane carriers (*Empress*, *Engadine* and *Riviera*) were used to launch seven seaplanes in an unsuccessful attack on the German Zeppelin base at Cuxhaven. This was, effectively, the world's first carrier-launched air strike. While seaplane carriers were primarily used as a tool for naval reconnaissance, the Royal Naval Air Service, which had been operating on the Western Front, also pushed for aircraft-carrying warships to accompany the fleet.

In early 1917, the light battlecruiser *Furious* was partially converted into an aircraft carrier, and on 2 August, the first carrier landing was carried out from it while the ship was under way in Scapa Flow. Although the pilot, Lt Cdr Dunning, was killed shortly afterwards, this paved the way for fully fledged carrier operations.

A Sopwith Pup pictured taking off from the port midships turret of the stationary battlecruiser HMS *New Zealand* in the spring of 1917. The flying-off ramp was a basic platform which could extend to the end of the gun barrels – a total length of just 60ft. Note the boat standing by, in case of accident.

In July 1918, seven Sopwith Camels took off from *Furious* and raided the German Zeppelin base at Tondern (now Tønder in Denmark), destroying two Zeppelins, for the loss of one fighter. With that, the age of naval aviation had truly arrived. In fact, it had already had an impact on the Grand Fleet. The Iron Duke-class dreadnoughts were the first British capital ships to be fitted with 2-pdr anti-aircraft (AA) guns, and by the end of the war most British warships carried some form of AA armament. The need for these weapons, though, was never properly tested in action.

HOW THE FLEET OPERATED

COMMAND AND ORGANIZATION

At the outbreak of war in August 1914, the British public, the press and indeed many officers and men in the Royal Navy expected a single climactic battle to take place, to finish the naval campaign in one conclusive test of arms. They had no doubt who would prevail. Everyone had high expectations of Britain's supremely powerful main battlefleet, and in the well-trained and well-led professionals who manned it – the officers and men who made up the crews of these dreadnoughts. Everyone had great pride in the Royal Navy, while the service itself was imbued with huge confidence, built in part on traditions dating back to the age of Nelson. One of these was a confident expectation of victory, regardless of the odds. There was no doubt that whatever the challenge, the Grand Fleet would acquit itself with honour and emerge victorious. However, as the months passed and the climactic clash never came, public disillusionment set in and pressure mounted to do something with the fleet. Few realized that it was doing its job perfectly well by supporting the economic blockade which was slowly winning the war without the need for a great clash of naval arms.

Admiral Sir John Jellicoe commanded the Grand Fleet from the outbreak of war in August 1914 until his move to the Admiralty in December 1916. His performance at Jutland was exemplary, but he was denied the clear victory he deserved thanks to the skill of his German counterpart.

The Strategic Situation

This of course, was only possible thanks to geography. The British Isles effectively blocked Germany's sea access to the rest of the world. The country lay like a giant barrier at the western side of the North Sea. There were only two ways past it. At the southern end, the Dover Straits were only 20 miles wide, and protected by mines, coastal batteries and warships. Even if the Germans penetrated these defences, they still had to run up the English Channel, the preserve of the Channel Fleet, and the

25

French Navy. The northern exit from the North Sea was much wider, stretching for 200 miles from Orkney and Shetland on one side, to the coast of southern Norway on the other. This too was covered by the minefields of the Northern Barrage, and by the cruisers of the Northern Patrol. Even more importantly, this route was also covered by the Grand Fleet, based in Scapa Flow. It acted, effectively, as the cork in the bottle, which kept the German High Seas Fleet penned up in its spacious but still constricting North Sea cage.

THE GRAND FLEET'S RESPONSE TO GERMAN SORTIES, 1914–18

The selection of Scapa Flow as a wartime base for the Grand Fleet was inspired, as it placed it beyond easy reach of attack, while giving it the ability to intercept any German sortie into the northern and central parts of the North Sea. It was considered unlikely that the German High Seas Fleet would conduct operations in the southern portion, below the shallow waters of Dogger Bank, as the geography restricted fleet movement, the area was mined by both sides and it rendered the Germans vulnerable to being cut off from their fleet base at Wilhelmshaven. Essentially, while it conducted occasional sweeps of its own or sortied to conduct limited offensive operations, the Grand Fleet was primarily retained in Scapa Flow, where it could react speedily to any German sortie.

For both Admiral Jellicoe and the British Admiralty, intelligence gathering was of vital importance. German wireless signals were relayed from a network of wireless direction stations on Britain's North Sea coast, and the information passed on to the Admiralty in London. There, in Room 40, these were analyzed, and the intelligence gathered passed on to the Admiralty and the Commander-in-Chief, Grand Fleet. This was further supported by submarine patrols, stationed off the Heligoland Bight, and by occasional naval patrols of the German side of the North Sea. From 1915, these were augmented by British naval airships. While these were primarily used for anti-submarine patrols or for convoy escort duties, they could also be deployed on maritime patrols. From 1917, specialist long-range patrol airships entered service, specifically designed for operations over the North Sea.

One of the main problems with the use of Scapa Flow was its distance from the German base at Wilhelmshaven, and the English coast south of Hull and the Humber Estuary. This diagram shows the radius of the fleet, in six-hour increments, when steaming at 20 knots. The main limiting factor was the fleet's attached destroyers, whose relatively short radius of operations meant that the Grand Fleet could only operate effectively as far as the southern edge of Dogger Bank or the Jutland Bank off the Danish coast. This equates to the '18-hour' radius shown here. To limit this restriction, the Battlecruiser Fleet was moved to Rosyth in the Firth of Forth, some 160 nautical miles south of Orkney. This meant that the battlecruiser fleet not only had a sizeable head start on the battlefleet, but it extended the radius of operations as far as the Dutch coast. By 1916, a battle squadron of the Grand Fleet was also stationed off Invergordon on the Cromarty Firth, some three to four hours' steaming closer to the central North Sea.

Co-ordinating any sortie of the Grand Fleet was conducted from the fleet flagship, using wireless. Signals were usually directed through a radio station at Cleethorpes, which linked the fleet commander with the Admiralty, the battlefleet to the battlecruiser fleet, and any other detached formations or scouting forces at sea. These included the Harwich Force, which regularly patrolled the southern portion of the North Sea and could be used to reinforce the Grand Fleet when necessary. All of this was still problematic, as by the time the fleet was at sea, intelligence was often out of date and the exact location of the enemy was unknown. In those cases, it was up to the fleet commander to deploy his scouting forces to give him the best chance of encountering the enemy, and then pinning it, so that the bulk of the Grand Fleet could concentrate its forces against its German counterparts.

The advantages of restricting the German High Seas Fleet were self-evident. First, it protected the movement of troops and supplies across the English Channel to France. Further afield it protected the world's sea lanes from German interference, and the transport of much-needed food and raw materials to Britain. The presence of the Grand Fleet protected the British coast from invasion across the North Sea, while the confinement of the German fleet also meant that it couldn't easily ship troops or supplies anywhere else in the world. Certainly, several German raiders were at sea, but their impact was relatively small, and they were all eventually hunted down. More serious was the growing U-boat threat, but that was essentially beyond the purview of the Grand Fleet. Despite all this though, the desire for a decisive sea battle remained, and would dominate naval strategy throughout the war.

For both the British Admiralty and Admiral Jellicoe, Commander-in-Chief of the newly constituted Grand Fleet, the strategic aims were clear. These were simply to block the two exits to the North Sea and seal the German battlefleet within its confines. There was an appreciation in British naval command that the maintenance of this blockade was the long-term key to victory in the war, and so the preservation of the Grand Fleet was therefore crucial to achieving this victory. While this didn't necessarily bring about a defensive stance by the fleet, it did encourage caution. This was particularly important given the German stratagem of *Kräfteausgleich* – the German intent to isolate and ambush detached elements of the British battlefleet, and so whittle down its strength. If this was the German stratagem, the British one was its avoidance. The destruction of the German battlefleet, while desirable, was of secondary importance to the preservation of the British one.

The Fleet Commander

In this respect, the choice of Admiral Sir John Jellicoe (1859–1935) as Commander-in-Chief of the Grand Fleet was an ideal one. He was unprepossessing in appearance – he was short, lean, balding and physically unremarkable. It could be said he looked like a mild-mannered middle-aged banker or civil servant, rather than a fighting admiral. What set Jellicoe apart though, was his personality and his intellect. He was a thoroughly capable professional, at the top of his game as a naval commander. He was kindly too – sometimes too much so, as it led to his supporting of subordinates who didn't match his own level of professional skill. However, he was extremely well liked by all of the men under his command, while his own staff described Jellicoe as inspiring, sincere, selfless and unflappable.

Above all though, he understood the task he had been given, and the strategic importance of both maintaining the blockade and preserving his battlefleet. Despite that, Jellicoe was as keen as anyone else to bring the enemy to battle if the opportunity presented itself. By the time the war broke out, naval officers had little training in strategy. Instead, they had a thorough grounding in tactics, in the capabilities of their ships and their weaponry, and in the complex manoeuvres and offensive or defensive measures required to fight a modern sea battle. Jellicoe went beyond that though. He had the rare ability to appraise a situation and deploy his fleet accordingly. On land, gifted commanders had an eye for the battlefield – the intuitive ability to know where to deploy their troops to best effect. Jellicoe had this too, only there was no terrain to appreciate – only the scrappy information gleaned from signals and the sight of his ships arrayed beside him. This gift came into its own at Jutland.

Jellicoe's deputy and eventual successor, Vice-Admiral Sir David Beatty (1871–1936), had this gift too. Beatty was a complex individual who was something of a man-about-town, wealthy socialite, sartorial dandy, sportsman, hunter and even dashing hero, having distinguished himself in action in Africa and China. He was never seen as a thorough professional like Jellicoe, but he was a highly competent naval commander. While he had little time for the details and technicalities of his trade, he had the ability to grasp the essentials and understand how they should be used to best effect. He was first and foremost a spirited leader, of exceptional self-reliance and belief, who was able to inspire his subordinates to follow his lead.

Vice-Admiral Sir David Beatty, commander of the Battlecruiser Fleet, and then, after his promotion in November 1916, Commander-in-Chief of the Grand Fleet. It was Beatty who accepted the surrender of the German High Seas Fleet two years later in November 1918.

The two men were totally different, but in a way they complemented each other – one the cautious and thoroughly professional commander, the other his dashing and aggressive subordinate, who seemed born into his role as commander of the Battlecruiser Fleet. In December 1916, Jellicoe handed over command of the fleet to Beatty and travelled to the Admiralty, to take up a new post as First Sea Lord. From then until the end of the war, Beatty commanded the fleet, and Jellicoe commanded Beatty. This though, made little significant difference to the course of the naval war. Beatty knew the task in hand and inherited a highly experienced staff to assist him.

Of course, what made things slightly simpler for both fleet commanders was that much of the decision-making process which one would normally expect from them was taken out of their hands. Instead, in all operational matters, they were controlled directly by the First Sea Lord and his War Staff, based in the Admiralty Building in London. On board the fleet flagship in Scapa Flow, Jellicoe and his staff were encouraged not to plan operations for themselves, save for hunts for potential German raiders or to support the Northern Patrol. Instead, the planning of strategic operations was very much the preserve of the Admiralty. It was a restrictive and authoritarian line of command, but for the most part it worked well.

The Admiralty

In theory, the Board of Admiralty in London was the highest level of command, and the group which Admiral Jellicoe reported to, as Commander-in-Chief of the Grand Fleet. It was from them that Jellicoe was given the ships, the manpower and the supplies his fleet needed to function. In practice though, the board were largely sidelined, and instead, all operational decisions regarding the Grand Fleet were made by one figure at the Admiralty – the First Sea Lord. He though, was one of the two leading figures on the Board of Admiralty.

The Board of Admiralty itself was made up of a mixture of senior naval officers, civil servants and politicians. Its chairman was the other leading figure in the command chain, the First Lord of the Admiralty. From 1911 until 1915, this key post was held by a politician, Winston Churchill, then a Liberal Cabinet Minister. A man of incredible energy, Churchill proved a dynamic figure, albeit one who kept dabbling in operational affairs – something outside his remit – regularly proposing novel ideas relating to everything from warship design to grand naval strategy. Fortunately, Churchill had a Naval Secretary on hand to advise him and to ameliorate some of his more outlandish ideas. From 1915 to 1916, the post was held by Arthur Balfour MP, who was succeeded by Edward Carson MP. He in turn was succeeded in 1917 by Eric Geddes MP, who remained in post until 1919.

The rest of the Board was made up of four admirals, three politicians and a civil servant. Two of the politicians were Civil Lords, responsible for the Admiralty's buildings and dockyards, while the third was the Political and Financial Secretary, who oversaw the Admiralty's budget. The four admirals were the Sea Lords, ranked First to Fourth, each with their own area of responsibility. The First Sea Lord, who in 1914 was the gifted Admiral Prince Louis of Battenberg, was in charge of naval operations, and so was the direct senior to Admiral Jellicoe. On 29 October 1914, and for the next seven months, the post was filled by Admiral of the Fleet Sir 'Jackie' Fisher, a brilliant but occasionally acerbic commander, who proved very supportive of Jellicoe during his tenure.

The Second Sea Lord, Vice-Admiral Sir Frederick Hamilton, the Third Sea Lord, Rear Admiral Sir Frederick Tudor and the Fourth Sea Lord, Commodore Cecil Lambert completed the board. Respectively they were responsible for manpower and training, ship design and construction, and naval supplies, and so had little say in the operational control of the Grand Fleet. The final member of the Board of Admiralty was its Permanent Secretary, a civil servant. Of all of these figures however, the key ones were the First Lord of the Admiralty, who shaped policy through his political

Admiral of the Fleet Sir John 'Jackie' Fisher, First Sea Lord from 1904 to 1910, and again from October 1914 until May 1915. In his first period in the role, he promoted the development of HMS *Dreadnought* and the creation of a dreadnought fleet.

connections, and the First Sea Lord, who effectively ran the operational side of the Royal Navy.

In operational matters, the First Sea Lord was assisted by a War Staff, responsible for the gathering of intelligence, naval mobilization and the protection of trade. These were essentially Admiralty divisions (departments), supervised by the Chief of the War Staff, Vice-Admiral Sir Doveton Sturdee. Each division had its head: the Director of Naval Intelligence, the Director (Operations Division), the Director (Mobilization Division) and the Director (Trade Division). From late 1916, other divisions were added, covering anti-submarine warfare, naval aviation, convoys and minesweeping. The Operations Division was also divided into 'Home' and 'Foreign' sections, and a communications section was added to deal with the transmission of orders.

Ceremonial small-arms drill being practised by Royal Marines on the afterdeck of the Royal Sovereign-class dreadnought HMS *Royal Oak* while lying at anchor in Scapa Flow in 1917. The senior officer in a cocked hat suggests the imminent arrival of some important visitor.

It all seemed incredibly complicated and cumbersome, but the War Staff were there to assist the First Sea Lord, making his job simpler by advising him on their relevant areas of expertise when required. For all operations undertaken by the Grand Fleet, the orders were issued by the First Sea Lord. In theory, he consulted the Board of Admiralty, but in practice all but the First Lord of the Admiralty were usually left out of the process. The First Sea Lord then, was the key figure, who effectively had full operational control over the Grand Fleet.

During the war, the First Sea Lord post changed several times:

THE FIRST SEA LORD, 1914–18
9 December 1912–29 October 1914: Admiral Prince Louis of Battenberg
29 October 1914–15 May 1915: Admiral of the Fleet Lord Fisher
15 May 1916–10 December 1916: Admiral Sir Henry Jackson
10 December 1916–10 January 1918: Admiral Sir John Jellicoe
10 January 1918–1 November 1919: Admiral Sir Rosslyn Wemyss

The main reason control of the Grand Fleet was so centralized was access to Naval Intelligence. The Naval Intelligence Division, thanks largely to its wireless interception section in Room 40 of the Admiralty, was able to monitor German naval activity, and so was aware of any German sortie almost as soon as it happened. In other words, the Admiralty had the most accurate intelligence of enemy naval movements possible – much more accurate than any available to the Commander-in-Chief of the Grand Fleet. So, this centralized command structure allowed the First Sea Lord and the War Staff to issue orders to the Grand Fleet extremely quickly. A secure wireless communication link had been established between the Admiralty and the Fleet Commander in Scapa Flow, and this was eventually augmented by a telephone link. As a result, the Grand

Fleet could put to sea almost as soon as the High Seas Fleet passed through the Jade Estuary in north-west Germany and entered the North Sea.

This reliance on Naval Intelligence collated in Room 40 proved increasingly important as the war went on. For instance, in December 1914, during the German raid on Scarborough, elements of the Grand Fleet were able to put to sea within hours and so were in a position to intercept the enemy. The same happened in January 1915, when the two forces clashed off Dogger Bank. The same was true during the German sorties against Lowestoft and Yarmouth in April 1916, the sortie that led to the battle of Jutland in May 1916, and then the later High Seas Fleet sortie that August. The timely receipt of intelligence was a key factor in all of these naval operations by the Grand Fleet, and in every case, the orders which sent the Grand Fleet to sea were issued directly by the First Sea Lord to Admiral Jellicoe and his subordinates.

The Admiral's Staff

Jellicoe of course had his own staff to advise him. When he first assumed command of the fleet, on 4 August 1914, he replaced Admiral Sir George Callaghan, Commander-in-Chief of the Home Fleet. One of his first moves after hoisting his flag in the dreadnought *Iron Duke* was to appoint his brother-in-law, Rear Admiral Charles E. Madden, as his Chief-of-Staff. It was an inspired choice. Madden was a quiet, reserved and intellectual officer, who had a thorough grasp of his profession. He was also a skilled tactician and was able to advise Jellicoe on the best deployment of the forces under his command. Madden's main weakness though, was his lack of imagination. For that, Jellicoe had to rely on others under his command. Thanks to the Admiralty, though, his opportunities for using his initiative were limited.

The dreadnought HMS *Iron Duke*, namesake of her class and fleet flagship of the Grand Fleet from the start of the war until January 1917, when the new fleet commander, Admiral Beatty, transferred his flag to HMS *Queen Elizabeth*. *Iron Duke* flies an admiral's flag at her foremast.

Jellicoe also inherited Admiral Callaghan's staff: a Captain of the Fleet, a Flag Captain and Flag Commander, a Wireless and two Signals Officers, two War Staff Officers and a Secretary. Later, Jellicoe would replace some of them with his own appointees: Commodore Halsey as Captain of the Fleet, Commander Forbes as Commander of the Fleet, and Fleet Paymasters Share and Weekes as Secretaries. Captain Lawson, the commander of *Iron Duke*, remained Flag Captain, and the two War Staff Officers – Commander Best and Lt Commander Bellairs – remained in post, as did the Signals Officers, Commander Woods and Lt Phipps, and Wireless

THE ORGANIZATION AND COMPOSITION OF THE GRAND FLEET, MAY 1916 (overleaf)

This diagram shows the organization of the Grand Fleet on the eve of the battle of Jutland, and its component commands. At this stage, Vice-Admiral Beatty's Battlecruiser Fleet was a semi-autonomous devolved command, although Beatty still took his orders directly from Admiral Jellicoe, Commander-in-Chief of the Grand Fleet. Each of the two elements, the Battlefleet and the Battlecruiser Fleet, contained a full cross-section of the fleet – capital ships, cruisers, destroyers and attendant vessels.

The core of the Battlefleet was its three squadrons of dreadnought battleships, each of eight warships. These squadrons were commanded by a vice-admiral, who also assumed command of a division of four dreadnoughts. The squadron was made up of two of these divisions, the second commanded by a rear admiral. These 24 dreadnoughts included HMS *Iron Duke*, the fleet flagship, which formed part of the 3rd Division of the 4th Battle Squadron. Jellicoe's flagship, while part of this formation, was something of a special case, as it was Jellicoe's orders, emanating from *Iron Duke*, which controlled not only the Battlefleet but the entire Grand Fleet. In the event Jellicoe was killed, command of the Grand Fleet would devolve to Beatty, while command of the Battlefleet would be transferred to the vice-admiral commanding the 1st Battle Squadron.

In normal circumstances, the 5th Battle Squadron, made up of the 'fast battleships' of the Queen Elizabeth class, would be attached to the Battlefleet. However, this divisional-sized force was on temporary attachment to the Battlecruiser Fleet. In exchange, the 3rd Battlecruiser Squadron was temporarily attached to the Battlefleet, shortly before the Jutland operation. There was no overall commander of cruisers in the Grand Fleet. Instead, the three cruiser squadrons were each commanded by a flag officer, who in turn reported directly to Jellicoe. The three destroyer flotillas attached to the Battlefleet were commanded by a Commodore of Flotillas, Grand Fleet, who also reported directly to Jellicoe. What would otherwise be a heavy burden on the Commander-in-Chief was eased slightly by the assistance of the Chief-of-Staff, Grand Fleet, who, together with a small staff, was embarked in Jellicoe's flagship.

The Battlecruiser Fleet was commanded by Vice-Admiral Beatty, who flew his flag in the battlecruiser HMS *Lion*. The Grand Fleet's battlecruisers were divided into three squadrons, one of which was temporarily attached to the Battlefleet shortly before Jutland. Beatty commanded the 1st Battlecruiser Squadron directly, while the 2nd Battlecruiser Squadron was led by a flag officer, who took his orders from Beatty. For the Jutland sortie, the 5th Battlecruiser Squadron was temporarily attached to the Battlecruiser Fleet, and again it was commanded by its own flag officer, who reported to Beatty. As in the Battlefleet, three light cruiser squadrons were attached to Beatty's command, each commanded by a flag officer or commodore, under the direct control of the flag officer, 3rd Light Cruiser Squadron, who in turn reported to Beatty. The three destroyer flotillas attached to the Battlecruiser Fleet (one of which was an amalgam of two smaller formations) were commanded by the senior captain, who was also commander of the 1st Flotilla. In the case of the 1st, 11th and 13th Flotillas, the leading ship of each flotilla was a light cruiser rather than a destroyer.

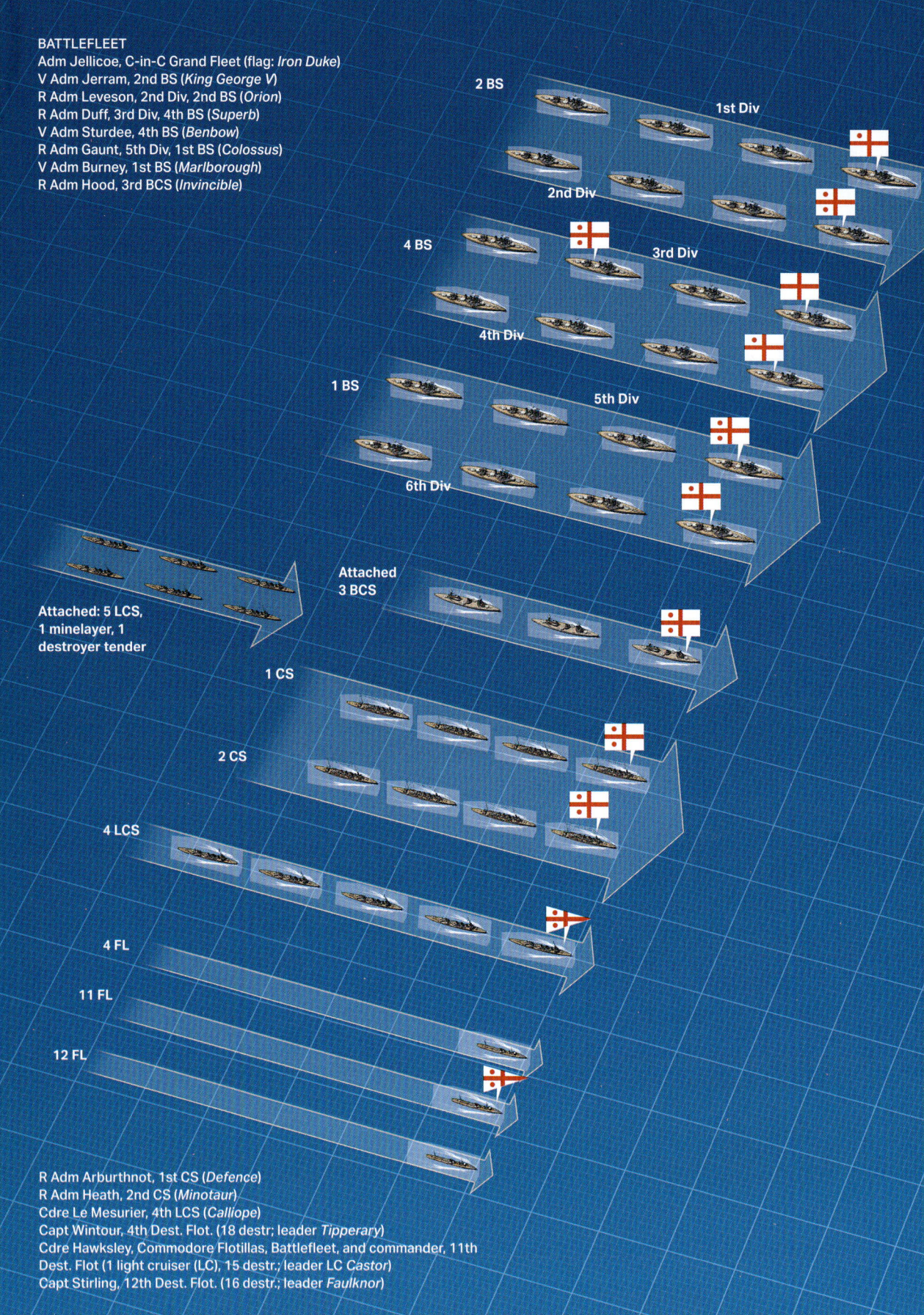

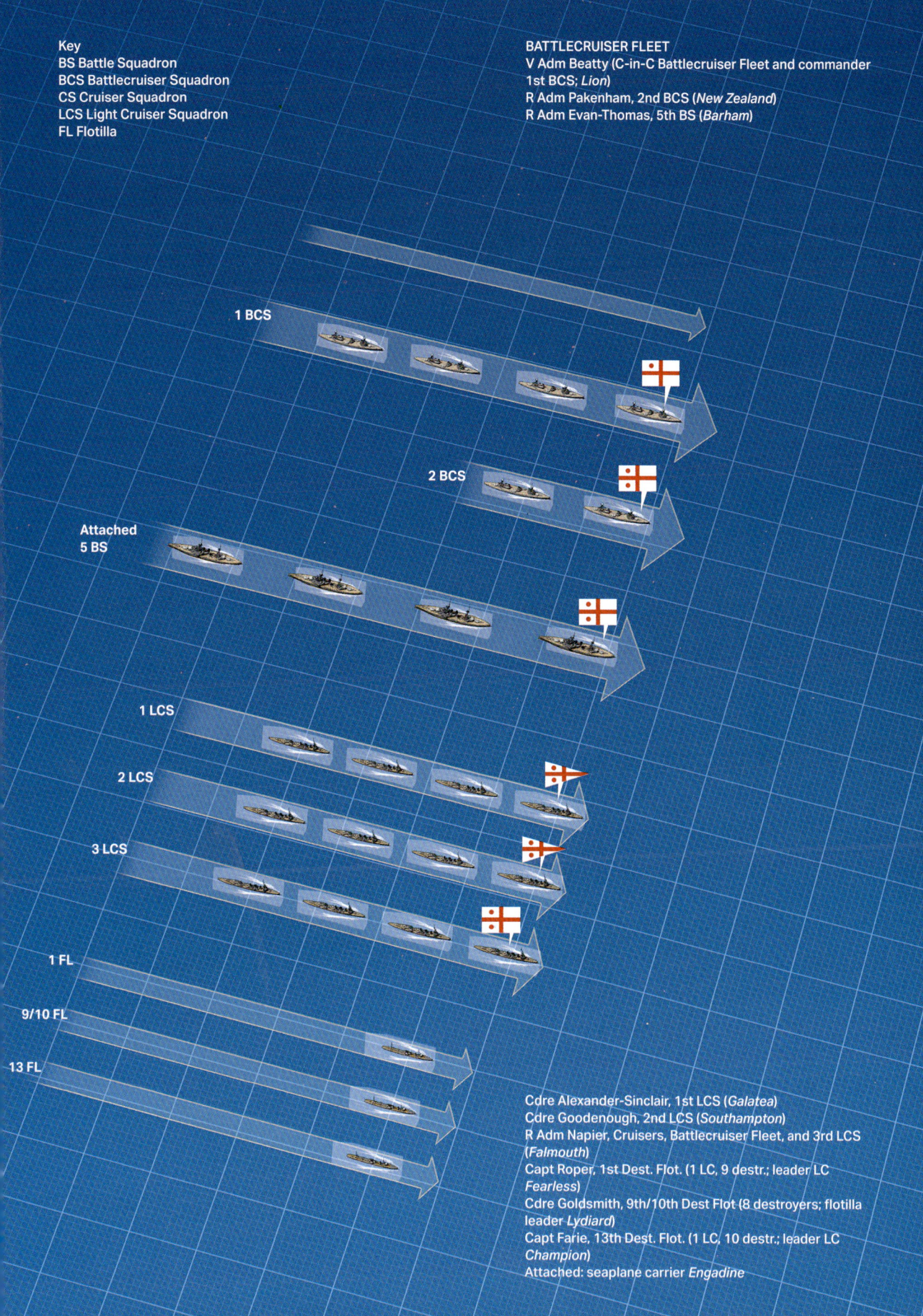

Warships of the Battlecruiser Fleet and the 2nd Battle Squadron, pictured at anchor in the Firth of Forth in early 1916 by a photographer in a British airship. The ships are anchored to the east of the Forth Rail Bridge, seen in the background. Rosyth Dockyard is further up the Forth, in the upper right of the photograph.

Officer Lt Commander Salmond. This staff increased slightly as the war progressed, but it was this small group of officers who helped shape Jellicoe's operational plans and helped him operate the fleet with skill and efficiency.

Fleet Organization

On 4 August 1914, on the orders of the Board of Admiralty, the British Home Fleet was renamed the Grand Fleet and now flew the flag of Admiral Sir John Jellicoe, the former Second Sea Lord. He had travelled from London to Orkney to assume the position of second-in-command of the Home Fleet, but upon his arrival, and following the outbreak of war, he opened sealed orders from the First Sea Lord which declared he was elevated to Commander-in-Chief of the newly created Grand Fleet with immediate effect. His predecessor, Sir George Callaghan, Commander-in-Chief of the Home Fleet, hauled down his flag and returned south. One of the first things Jellicoe did upon assuming the post was to survey his command.

The peacetime Home Fleet, now the wartime Grand Fleet, was centred around the battlefleet of 19 dreadnought battleships, in three squadrons. More dreadnoughts were due to enter service, and would join the fleet's 4th Battle Squadron as soon as they could. In the meantime, the eight 'pre-dreadnought' battleships of the 3rd Battle Squadron formed part of the fleet. The 'wobbly eight', as they were known – for their poor stability in rough weather – were something of a liability in a clash with German dreadnoughts, but for the moment they were needed to make up numbers. It would have been some consolation to Jellicoe that his German counterpart, Admiral von Ingenohl, also had to bulk out his battlefleet with pre-dreadnoughts. Ideally though, pre-dreadnoughts were to be kept out of danger, the British ones in the English Channel and the German ones in the Baltic Sea.

The second-in-command of the battlefleet was Vice-Admiral Sir Douglas Gamble, who commanded the still-incomplete 4th Battle Squadron. The other three battle squadrons were also commanded by a vice-admiral (Sir Lewis Bayly of the 1st Battle Squadron, Sir George Warrender of the 2nd and Edward Bradford of the 3rd). Each of these three commanders was competent enough, but lacked initiative. This was rarely a problem though, as the battle squadrons all formed part of a highly regulated larger entity – the battlefleet. The exception was Bayly, who, later in the war, had the ability to hold independent command – something he achieved while countering the German U-boat threat.

Typically, a fully formed battle squadron was made up of eight dreadnoughts, which were divided in turn into two divisions, each of up to four ships. While the vice-admiral commanding the battle squadron commanded the whole, as well as one of the two divisions, his deputy, a rear admiral, commanded the remaining division in the squadron. In 1914, these 'rear flags' were Hugh Evan-Thomas of the 1st Squadron, Sir Robert Arbuthnot of the 2nd and Montague Browning of the 3rd. For the moment, Vice-Admiral Gamble of the 4th Battle Squadron had no deputy, as he only had three dreadnoughts in his understrength command.

Jellicoe's second-in-command was Vice-Admiral Sir David Beatty, who commanded the 1st Battlecruiser Squadron. Unlike the other vice-admirals in the battlefleet, Beatty could be expected to have other formations temporarily attached to his command in order to lead scouting operations ahead of the battlefleet. These for the most part would be drawn from the fleet's cruiser squadrons and destroyer flotillas. The two cruiser squadrons, made up of armoured cruisers, usually accompanied the battlefleet. Each was commanded by a rear admiral, the Honourable Somerset Gough-Calthorpe of the 2nd Cruiser Squadron (CS) and William Packenham of the 2nd CS. That left Commodore William Goodenough's 1st Light Cruiser Squadron (LCS) eligible for attachment to the battlecruisers. Again, other battlecruisers and light cruisers were serving elsewhere when the war began, and so when these became available to the Grand Fleet, it was likely that the fleet would undergo a degree of reorganization, to accommodate them.

In addition, the Grand Fleet contained two destroyer flotillas made up of modern destroyers, each commanded by a captain, whose flotilla leader was either a purpose-built destroyer leader – a destroyer with improved staff and accommodation facilities – or a small cruiser. In August 1914, the fleet also included a small force of minelayers, although for the most part these were fully engaged in the creation of the Northern Barrage minefield between Orkney and Norway. Also attached to the Grand Fleet was the 10th Cruiser Squadron, also known as the Northern Patrol, which was responsible for enforcing the blockade in these same waters. They though, were detached from the Grand Fleet, and for the most part were based in Kirkwall.

The core of the fleet, though, was its battlefleet. While commanded directly by Jellicoe in his fleet flagship *Iron Duke*, it was invariably deployed in its individual battle squadrons, with each either in a single line ahead or in a pair of divisional-sized columns. Squadron and fleet manoeuvres were routinely

The forecastle of the dreadnought HMS *King George V*, namesake of her class, as her crew line the side for a visit from King George V in the aftermath of the surrender of the German fleet in 1918. This view shows the deflection scale painted on the side of 'B' turret, to simplify fire control.

practised, with station-keeping considered of prime importance. The real value of the dreadnought lay in its main armament, which was best employed when firing a full salvo to either beam. So for Jellicoe, while columns of either squadrons or divisions made progress easier when at sea, if an engagement was expected then it was important to redeploy the battlefleet into a single battle line, with all of the dreadnoughts capable of firing their broadsides as a single entity. This was the primary aim of the fleet commander in a naval battle – to make the most of his dreadnoughts' combined weight of firepower.

When conducting a sweep in the North Sea, the battlefleet was usually preceded by light forces – the battlecruisers and light cruisers. For the most part, heavy cruisers were retained in a supporting role to counter unexpected attacks by enemy light forces. The destroyer flotillas were kept together too, ready to be launched at an enemy battlefleet if a suitable opportunity arose. When the fleet expanded, and Beatty was given command of the Battlecruiser Fleet, the principle remained the same. Despite being based at Rosyth on the Firth of Forth, these stayed under Jellicoe's overall command, but would be commanded directly by Beatty from his own fleet flagship, the battlecruiser *Lion*.

The battlecruiser squadrons would act as support for the scouting line of light cruisers as Beatty attempted to locate the enemy fleet at sea. Then, once contact was made, the battlecruisers would support the lighter forces and attempt to engage the enemy, as would any attached destroyer flotillas. Above all though, Beatty's Battlecruiser Fleet was the scouting arm of the Grand Fleet. So, its primary purpose was to locate the enemy, and then guide the Grand Fleet's battlefleet into contact with them, ideally in a position which was advantageous to Jellicoe's dreadnoughts. This, despite Beatty's other shortcomings that day, is what Beatty achieved successfully at the battle of Jutland, on 31 May 1916.

INTELLIGENCE, COMMUNICATION AND DECEPTION

Almost every sortie of the Grand Fleet during the war took place as a result of intelligence reports of a German sortie from Wilhelmshaven. This meant that the operation was invariably initiated by the Admiralty in London, rather than by the fleet commander. Once at sea though, the Commander-in-Chief, Grand Fleet, was generally left to conduct the operation as he saw fit. However, Jellicoe was frequently irritated by interference from the Admiralty, with orders being issued directly from them to his subordinates – most usually to Beatty and his Battlecruiser Fleet, or to the commander of the 2nd Battle Squadron when it was based in the Cromarty Firth, rather than in Scapa Flow. When Jellicoe challenged the Admiralty on this interference in the protocols of the naval chain of command, the Admiralty usually replied that their direct orders were the result of fresh intelligence of enemy ship movements. For them, the speed of response by the fleet's subordinate commanders was considered more important than maintaining the proper channels. This demonstrates two things – the degree sorties by the Grand Fleet were largely directed by the Admiralty, and the importance of timely intelligence on German naval movements.

Communications

The development of wireless communications was extremely rapid before the war. The first short-range wireless signal was sent in 1885, and by the end of the century, transmissions had been sent across the English Channel. A year later, a

When she entered service in July 1917, the light battlecruiser HMS *Furious* had already been modified into a hybrid aircraft carrier, with a partial flight deck forward. In December 1917, she was converted into a full carrier, rejoining the Grand Fleet in March 1918. That July, Sopwith Camels launched from *Furious* attacked the German Zeppelin sheds at Tondern (now Tønder).

signal was sent across the Atlantic. This was a long way, though, from providing a reliable form of transmission which could be used by ships at sea. Still, guided by the Admiralty, experiments were begun in 1900, using a stationary lightship. The following year, the Royal Navy began testing the first short-range wireless sets aboard its warships. During torpedo exercises in 1904, a destroyer flotilla commander used wireless to gather his vessels, which had become scattered in fog. By this stage, merchant ships had also begun to adopt wireless sets, as both range and reliability improved steadily.

The Royal Navy led the way in the development of naval wireless, and by 1914 most Royal Naval warships carried wireless sets, operated from their own wireless transmission (W/T) offices. Before the war, Admiral Fisher had developed the control of battlefleets through the use of wireless, although the range of signals remained a problem until the eve of war. For longer-range signals, a network of wireless signal stations allowed signals to be broadcast across much larger distances. Conversely, in wartime, the destruction of enemy wireless signal stations would limit the enemy's ability to transmit signals to their overseas possessions and naval units in distant waters. By August 1914, wireless was widely used at sea, and it was a wireless signal sent early on 5 August 1914, that notified all British-flagged ships at sea that Britain was now at war with Imperial Germany.

During this period, naval wireless signals were sent using Morse Code, usually but not always in an encoded form. The Grand Fleet and Battlecruiser Fleet commanders were both assigned their own radio frequencies for long-range communications with the Admiralty, by way of a powerful land-based transmitter at Cleethorpes on the Lincolnshire coast. This was later extended to squadron commanders. During North Sea operations, each squadron flagship would listen out on these frequencies (or 'tunes', as they were often called), for set periods each hour or continually during close action. The Grand Fleet also used a dedicated Destroyer Wave, to co-ordinate the deployment of its flotillas. For communications within the ships of a squadron, short-wave radio signals were used. The fleet also had a dedicated W/T guardship, which would pass on signals from the Admiralty to the relevant flagships in case they were missed. This was important, as the powerful spark radio systems used during this period were prone to interference from other users if several ships were transmitting signals simultaneously.

For the most part, signals used by warships for communications within a fleet were restricted to short range, to reduce the risk of their interception. The Royal Navy were also well aware that signals could be intercepted by the enemy, so frequencies and call signs were varied, especially if operations were considered imminent. For the most part though, Jellicoe preferred to rely wherever possible on other means of signalling. Each warship carried signal lamps, which were considered more reliable than communicating using hoists of signal flags; these still carried the risk of being intercepted by enemy ships. A naval signal lamp had a range of around 4 nautical miles at night – twice its daylight distance, and at Jutland, both sides were able to see nocturnal enemy lamp signals during the battle, which gave away the signallers' presence.

However, given the distances involved in naval warfare during this period, it wasn't always possible to maintain radio silence. In fact, at times a steady flow of wireless signals was a necessity. For instance, at Jutland, when the Battlecruiser Fleet first made contact with its German counterparts, and then sighted the German battlefleet, the wireless signals sent by British warships gave Jellicoe the information he needed to deploy his battlefleet across the path of the enemy. Conversely, the radio silence his standing orders demanded proved a hindrance during the night battle that followed and played a part in allowing the German battlefleet to escape destruction. Wireless then, was a vital naval tool during the war, but it carried with it some limitations. The most significant of these was the risk of the signals being intercepted by the enemy. While attempts at signal jamming were in their infancy, as a means of disrupting enemy operations, the sole means of screening friendly transmissions was limited to the encoding of signals. So, naval intelligence work was centred on the interception of these encrypted signals, and their decoding.

Naval Intelligence

The Admiralty's Naval Intelligence Division (NID) was created in 1912. It had evolved from the Victorian era's Naval Intelligence Department, which had further responsibilities, but by 1914 these had been transferred to other departments. So, the wartime NID was solely responsible for the gathering of intelligence, its analysis and the dissemination of this information to the necessary people. In 1914, it was headed by Rear Admiral Henry Oliver, a member of the Admiralty's War Staff, who reported directly to the First Sea

The sleek battlecruiser HMS *Princess Royal* was the sister ship of Beatty's flagship, HMS *Lion*, and during the war served in the 1st Battlecruiser Squadron. She saw action off Heligoland (1914) and at Dogger Bank (1915) and Jutland (1916), when she was hit by nine large-calibre shells, but remained in the fight throughout the battle.

Lord. Oliver had held the post since the previous December, but in November 1914, this experienced but reticent and somewhat dour Scottish Borderer was made the Secretary to the First Lord of the Admiralty, Winston Churchill. As his 'sea daddy', as it were, his new role was to advise Churchill on naval matters, and to patiently explain the workings of the service to him. Oliver also became the Chairman of the Admiralty's War Staff. From 14 November, Oliver's post as Director, Intelligence Department (DID) was assumed by Commodore Reginald Hall (1870–1943).

'Blinker' Hall was an inspired choice, even though he was appointed on Oliver's recommendation largely due to his poor health, which, after the battle of Heligoland Bight that August, had led to him giving up command of the battlecruiser *Queen Mary*. Despite his strong religious convictions, Hall was something of a free thinker and had already established a reputation as an innovator. One of his first tasks in the NID was to establish a cryptanalysis section, which was established in Room 40 of the Old Admiralty Building in Whitehall. In fact, the first steps towards the analysis of German signal codes had already been undertaken by Oliver the month before, when he enlisted the help of the Director of Naval Education, Alfred Ewing, to see if he could decrypt German naval wireless traffic emanating from the German Naval High Command in Berlin.

Under Hall's encouragement, Ewing recruited other civilians to assist him, including Alexander 'Alistair' Denniston, a sportsman and German linguist, Nigel de Grey, headhunted from the publishing house of Heinemann, the Cambridge classicist Dillwyn Cox and the Rev William Montgomery, a translator of German theological works. Soon, German wireless intercepts gathered from a receiving station at Stockton-on Tees as well as other commercial wireless stations were passed on to Room 40 for analysis. The grounding of the German light cruiser *Magdeburg* in the Baltic in late August 1914 gave this ad hoc team the break it needed. The cruiser's naval signal and code books were captured by the Russian Navy, which duly passed one on to the British Admiralty in mid-October. The Germans thought that the books had been destroyed, and so didn't change their signal codes.

A second signals and code book, recovered by the Royal Australian Navy from a German merchantman, also helped the cryptanalysis team. Here though, although the Germans knew their signals books had been captured, they remained unchanged until 1916. As a result of these two captured books, and a third recovered from a German destroyer sunk off the Dutch coast near Texel later that year, the team in Room 40 were able to decipher most German naval wireless signals. By the end of 1914, the flow of cryptanalysis information from the NID was enough to give the Admiralty a fairly accurate picture of the movements of the German High Seas Fleet. They knew, for instance, when the fleet put to sea or gathered off Wilhelmshaven, in the Jade River Estuary, waiting for the signal to proceed to sea.

The activities of the Room 40 team were top secret, but the sheer volume of information they intercepted and decoded threatened to overwhelm the small department. So, Cdr Herbert Hope was appointed to analyse the wireless intercepts and apply his naval expertise to them. As a result, from early 1915 on, the intelligence-gathering system was greatly improved, with key intercepts given priority over more routine signals. As Hope answered directly to both Hall and the First Sea Lord, there was no delay in bringing this vital information to those in the Admiralty who made the operational decisions. As a result, within an hour of a vital signal being decoded, the First Sea Lord could be issuing orders to the Grand Fleet to put to sea.

It was thanks to the cryptanalysis of Room 40 that the Grand Fleet was able to react to the German sorties which led to the bombardment of Hartlepool, Scarborough and Whitby in late 1914, the sortie which led to the battle of Dogger Bank in early 1915, the raid on Lowestoft in the spring of 1916 and the German sortie towards the Skagerrak that May that resulted in the battle of Jutland. Despite the changing of German naval codes, Room 40 continued to gather vital information, which led to the Grand Fleet putting to sea in August 1916, and again later in the war. Without this flow of high-quality naval intelligence, or the work of wireless direction-finding units, Admiral Jellicoe would have been poorly placed to respond to German naval movements. Certainly, other sources of information existed, including through the espionage work of military intelligence, sighting reports of British submarines on patrol off the Heligoland Bight, and even reports by foreign embassies and armed forces. None of them though, matched the intelligence gathered by Room 40 and the NID.

Another useful form of intelligence gathering was also achieved by wireless intercepts. During the war, a number of wireless direction stations were established along Britain's North Sea coast, from South Ronaldsay in Orkney down to Flamborough Head, between Scarborough and Hull. Each recorded the bearing of an intercepted German signal, and these were duly passed to the Admiralty, where the information was gathered. It was a simple matter to compare the bearings on a chart, and so see where these intersected. This would give the approximate position of the transmitting vessel. Signals Intelligence (or Sigint) then, gleaned from wireless direction stations, became an important part of Britain's intelligence-gathering network.

The Iron Duke-class dreadnought HMS *Marlborough*, pictured in the Firth of Forth in mid-1918 while launching a kite balloon from her quarterdeck. These observation balloons were designed to be used to extend the sighting range of a battlefleet, but practical problems when flying them from warships steaming at speed proved hard to overcome.

The Grand Fleet's battlefleet at anchor in the main fleet anchorage, Scapa Flow. In the foreground are the small picket boats and ships' boats which were regularly moving around the anchorage, as well as a trawler, one of many taken into service to bring supplies to the fleet or to man Scapa Flow's booms and torpedo nets. (painting by William L. Wyllie)

This meant that once units of the High Seas Fleet put to sea, if they transmitted using wireless sets – either from surface ships, surfaced U-boats or Zeppelins – the British would quickly learn their location. Passing this information on quickly was key, so bearings were sent for plotting as soon as they took place, and the resulting information passed on to the fleet by the Admiralty soon afterwards. If the fleet was at sea, the information was then sent by wireless to the fleet flagship, by way of the Navy's powerful transmitting station at Cleethorpes. As a result, plots derived from wireless directions stations could reach Jellicoe's flagship within an hour of the signal first being received.

During the war there was little attempt at deception in naval operations. This was limited to the sending of false signals by both sides, reporting the departure of naval units, or their safe return. The aim, of course, was to entice the enemy fleet to sea, where it could potentially fall into a trap – either a waiting line of U-boats, a secretly aid minefield, or a waiting battlefleet. For some reason though, this was rarely done. Naval Intelligence was more about the gathering of intelligence than the use of deception. In fact, both sides were active in the monitoring of enemy radio traffic, which yielded information such as the sweeping of enemy minefields, the deployment of submarines or U-boats and the putting to sea of major formations. The same tool could have been more widely used to disseminate false information. However, apart from the use of special codes to deceive listeners, this was an area which both the British and the Germans failed to exploit.

BASES AND LOGISTICS

In times of peace, the Royal Navy used its long-established bases at Portsmouth and Plymouth, together with secondary bases at Chatham and Rosyth. Other smaller bases were also employed, but the bulk of naval facilities and logistical support activity was concentrated in the two great south-coast ports. Each warship in the fleet had its own 'home port', which equated to one of these four main naval bases, so the support train for these ships, from spare parts and supplies to the housing of families and shore administrative facilities, was concentrated there. The move of the Home Fleet to Scapa Flow on the eve of the outbreak of war ended this long-established relationship between ship and base. Instead, the ships and men of the Home Fleet, or the Grand Fleet as it became when war was declared, now had to rely far more on themselves, augmented by whatever nascent facilities Scapa Flow could provide.

For centuries, when France was Britain's most likely enemy, basing the fleet at Portsmouth and Plymouth made sense. However, war with Germany, where the North Sea would be the battleground required a different base – one closer to the action, and which couldn't be so easily blocked up by the German mining of the Dover Straits. After the war, Lord Fisher claimed to have selected Scapa Flow, but in fact this spacious natural harbour had already been used occasionally by the Royal Navy. So, in the early 20th century, when the Admiralty considered the strategic implications of a war with Germany, and it sought a suitable base on the North Sea coast, the value of Scapa Flow was already known. The Admiralty considered other options, such as the Cromarty Firth, the Firth of Forth and the Humber Estuary. All these, however, shared the same drawback: they only had one entrance, which could easily be blocked by enemy mines.

Two of these places would later be used by the Grand Fleet as secondary bases. However, only Scapa Flow had more than one entrance, which made it extremely difficult to block. It also lay beyond the reach of a surprise attack by the enemy, of the kind the Japanese had achieved in 1904 against Port Arthur, the Russian naval base in the Pacific. With two main entrances, at Hoxa Sound and Hoy Sound, Scapa Flow was hard to attack, especially when one took into account the Pentland Firth, where strong currents, rocky skerries and turbulent eddies made the approach through Hoxa Sound something of a navigational hazard. The anchorage itself was relatively deep-watered and commodious. It was also close to the northern exit from the North Sea, and so was ideally placed to ensure the German fleet was contained. In other words, Scapa Flow perfectly suited the needs of the Admiralty.

The only problem was that in August 1914, Scapa Flow was completely undefended. Jellicoe was appalled, and immediately landed small guns to overlook the two entrances and create temporary coastal batteries. These were bolstered by destroyer patrols, while old merchant ships were purchased, then scuttled across the smaller entrances on the eastern side of Scapa Flow – Water Sound, Weddel Sound and Kirk Sound. While no anti-submarine nets were available, fishing nets were purchased and suspended across the main channels from lines of buoys. The threat was real enough. On 9 August, a German U-boat was spotted on the surface, to the north of Orkney. The quick-thinking captain of the light cruiser HMS *Birmingham* rammed and sank the boat, U-15, but it showed that Scapa Flow was well within range of these boats.

The following month, nervous crews thought that a U-boat had penetrated the anchorage, and shot at anything suspicious, including seals. The 'first battle of Scapa Flow' was something of an embarrassment,

At the outbreak of the war, Scapa Flow was defenceless. As a short-term measure, light guns were landed from the fleet and set up to command the seaward approaches to the anchorage. Here, a naval crew man a 3-pdr (1.85in. or 47mm) quick-firing Vickers gun mounted on the shore of Flotta, overlooking Switha Sound.

but it underlined the need for adequate defences. As a result, Jellicoe spent most of the next few weeks at sea until the base's defences could be strengthened. Afterwards, Jellicoe summed up the severity of the threat:

> The conclusion generally held by experienced submarine officers was that, whilst the least important entrances, such as the Hoy, the Switha and the Holm Sound Channels, would be extremely difficult for the passage of a submarine, entry by the Hoxa Sound Channel was quite practicable by a determined submarine officer … The anxiety of officers in command of Fleets or Squadrons at anchor in any of the Bases used by the Grand Fleet was immense. For my part, I was always far more concerned for the safety of the Fleet when it was at anchor in Scapa Flow during the exceedingly brief periods which were spent there for coaling in the early days of the War, than I was when the Fleet was at sea, and this anxiety was reflected in the very short time that the Fleet was kept in harbour.

This emphasis on 'any of the Bases' reflects that at this early stage of the war, the same lack of defences also made the fleet's secondary bases in the Cromarty Firth and the Firth of Forth equally vulnerable. Jellicoe also considered the situation from the German perspective:

> I have often wondered why the Germans did not make greater efforts to reduce our strength in capital ships by destroyer or submarine attacks on our bases in those early days. They possessed, in comparison with the uses for which they were required, almost a superfluity of destroyers, certainly a superfluity as compared with ourselves, and they could not have put them to a better use than in an attack on Scapa Flow during the early months of the 1914–1915 winter.

Eventually, 15 'blockships' were scuttled in the small entrances on the eastern side of Scapa Flow, blocking off these approaches. Five more were sunk on

The Grand Fleet at anchor in Scapa Flow, viewed from the north. The battlefleet is lying in the main fleet anchorage off the island of Flotta, on the left, with the small Calf of Flotta in the bottom left. In the background lie the smaller islands of Fara and Cava, with the much larger and more rugged island of Hoy. (watercolour by William L. Wyllie)

Much of the daily routine of the British sailor on board a warship in Scapa Flow involved tasks such as scrubbing the deck, chipping or painting, repairing wire or cordage, and making other repairs around the sailors' assigned part of the ship. Here, a working party scrub the deck of a dreadnought, possibly HMS *Emperor of India*.

the western side of Scapa Flow, in Burra Sound, between the islands of Hoy and Graemsay. These were augmented by steel anti-submarine obstacles. Next, booms were laid across Hoxa Sound between the islands of South Ronaldsay and Flotta, and Switha Sound, another narrow entrance nearby, between Flotta and the southern tip of Hoy. A third boom was strung across Bring Deeps, a passage to the east of Hoy Sound, between the Orkney mainland and Hoy. Trawlers were converted into boom vessels, to open and close these booms when warships needed to pass through the channels.

Next, shore batteries were built, overlooking the three booms, with another sited at Ness Point, overlooking Hoy Sound, and one covering the approaches to Kirk Sound, on the eastern side of Orkney. A final battery was built covering the approaches to Kirkwall Bay, the base of the Northern Patrol. In all, nine batteries were established, which effectively rendered Scapa Flow secure from surface attack. That left the anti-submarine defences. Controlled minefields were laid in front of Bring Deeps, and in Hoxa Sound and Switha Sound, which could be activated from the shore if a U-boat was detected trying to enter the anchorage. In addition, magnetic inductor loops were laid on the seabed outside the seaward ends of Hoxa Sound and Hoy Sound, to detect any submerged U-boat which attempted the same feat. Finally, a string of searchlight batteries dotted the coast, to spot any attempt to sneak into Scapa Flow under cover of darkness. All this took time, though, and it was almost a year after the start of the war before all these defences were finally in place and Scapa Flow was regarded as completely secure.

When the war began, the main fleet anchorage was at Scapa Bay, in the northern part of Scapa Flow. A pier at Scapa was used as the temporary fleet headquarters and allowed easy access to Orkney's main town, Kirkwall, just over a mile away to the north. By early 1915 though, the main anchorage was moved to just to the north of Flotta, on the south-western side of Scapa Flow.

This area, bounded to the south by the northern side of Flotta, and to the west by the smaller islands of Fara and Cava was eventually protected by torpedo nets, and later in the war barrage balloons were added, in the unlikely event the enemy would attempt a long-range Zeppelin bombing raid on the fleet anchorage. In all, the main fleet anchorage covered an area of some 5 square nautical miles – more than enough to accommodate the battlefleet and most of the fleet's cruisers.

Additional anchorage areas were situated to the north, off the Orkney mainland near Houton – an area which in 1918–19 would be occupied by the interned German High Seas Fleet. For the most part, destroyers were anchored on the far side of Fara and Cava, between these islands and the larger island of Hoy. This placed them close to the fleet's main shore base at Lyness on Hoy. It was clear that administering the base was beyond Jellicoe's remit. So, Vice-Admiral Sir Henry Colville was appointed as Flag Officer, Orkney and Shetland, to oversee the defence of Scapa Flow, and the naval base and facilities established there. He was supported by Rear Admiral Miller, who dealt with the administrative side of the base at Lyness and the support facilities established for use by the fleet.

Inevitably, at the start of the war, Scapa Flow was bare of the infrastructure and facilities needed to turn the place into a fully operational naval base. When it

SCAPA FLOW – THE ANCHORAGE OF THE GRAND FLEET

The potential of Scapa Flow as a naval base had been recognized during the Napoleonic Wars, and Britain's Victorian fleet used the place as an anchorage during summer manoeuvres. However, it only became a wartime naval base on the eve of World War I. In June 1914, the Grand Fleet began its redeployment there, and the defences of the anchorage were strengthened. But, it would be mid-1915 before these defences were fully complete.

Scapa Flow was a vast natural deep-water anchorage, large enough to accommodate the entire Grand Fleet, yet was sufficiently landlocked to render it relatively easy to defend. It had two main entrances, through Hoxa Sound in the south, leading into the Pentland Firth, and the smaller Hoy Sound to the west, which led directly into the Atlantic Ocean. Both of these entrances were protected by boom defences and coastal batteries. The threat posed by U-boats led to these surface defences being augmented by induction loops to detect enemy submarines, controlled minefields, which could be activated when a U-boat entered them, and anti-torpedo nets, rigged around the main fleet anchorage.

This diagram shows where Scapa Flow was situated, to the north of the island of Flotta. Shore facilities were built at Lyness in Hoy, with a naval headquarters sited nearby, while repair and maintenance ships were anchored off Lyness and additional facilities were established ashore. Direct communication with the Admiralty in London was provided by phone and wireless links, ensuring the fleet commander remained fully apprised of any naval intelligence reports. What the anchorage lacked, at least for much of the war, were recreation facilities to help entertain the warship crews. This, and the often bleak and challenging weather in winter, made Scapa Flow an unpopular posting for many. However, a steamer to Scrabster on the southern side of the Pentland Firth served as a link to the railhead at Thurso, allowing a steady flow of mail and newspapers, and the transport of sailors to and from leave. For much of the war, though, these men remained aboard their ships, at anchor in Scapa Flow, waiting for the Germans to put to sea.

Wreck of HMS *Hampshire* 1916
N
E
S
Hoy Sound
Stromness
ORKNEY MAINLAND
GAIRSAY
SHAPINSAY
Kirkwall
Key
Coastal Battery
Boom
Blockship
Controlled Minefield (submerged)
Induction Loop (submerged)
GRAEMSAY
Scapa Bay
HOY
CAVA
SCAPA FLOW
Main Fleet
Wreck of HMS *Vanguard* 1917
FARA
Lyness Naval base
FLOTTA
BURRAY
COPINSAY
Naval HQ
SWITHA
St Margaret's Hope
NORTH SEA
SOUTH RONALDSAY
PENTLAND FIRTH
Wrecks of HMS *Opal* and *Narborough* 1918
SWONA
0
5 Miles
10

arrived there, the fleet was accompanied by the fleet repair ship HMS *Assistance*, whose crew and working parties from other ships were set to work establishing defences and to assist in the establishment of coaling facilities for the fleet at Lyness. Base ships were used to support the fleet, anchored off Lyness and the small village of Longhope to the south, where Jellicoe established a small shore headquarters in the local hotel. Colliers, store ships, repair ships, hospital ships and ammunition ships also appeared, and were berthed close to Lyness or the main fleet anchorage off Flotta. In late September 1914, a floating dry dock also arrived from Portsmouth, to permit the dockage of destroyers and the smaller cruisers. Jellicoe also ensured wireless communications were improved, and a land link established, which allowed the sending of secure signals between the Admiralty and Scapa Flow.

Gradually then, during the winter of 1914–15, Scapa Flow became the self-sufficient fleet anchorage it was meant to be. A regular flow of supply ships meant that the crews could enjoy plentiful rations, including fresh meat and vegetables, and of course rum for the men's daily ration. These, where possible, were augmented by provisions purchased locally, from farmers grateful for the business.

For most crews though, there was little contact with anything outside their ship. Instead they lay anchored in Scapa Flow, each an isolated floating world in itself. Both Jellicoe and his captains tried to fill the days with drills and exercises, while each ship had its own routine of maintenance, painting and repair. In the long winters though, it was much harder, and gales and rain lashed the decks, and the crew avoided the upper deck. Inter-ship sports flourished, with boxing, boat racing, and later, once pitches and sports facilities were established on Flotta and Lyness, with football, rugby and even golf and tennis. Amenities on Flotta though, were minimal until 1916, and just consisted of a hut, which served tea to the sportsmen. Eventually though, facilities were improved, as bars, cafeterias and recreation huts were built.

When the Grand Fleet first arrived in Scapa Flow in August 1914, it anchored in Scapa Bay at the northern end of the large and enclosed harbour. Here, pre-dreadnought battleships, cruisers and supply ships can be seen, lying off its eastern shore.

Coaling was usually undertaken by colliers coming alongside each beam of a warship, and all hands were ordered to coal ship. This filthy, back-breaking work was unavoidable though, and usually 2,000 tons were taken aboard a dreadnought, to ensure the ship was ready for sea at all times. The inclusion of oil-fired ships required the building of oil tanks near Lyness, while others were also built at Invergordon and Rosyth. Fuel pumping with the vessel tied alongside a fuel jetty, was a much less onerous business than taking on coal. Every few months, a warship was sent to Scapa Bay, at the northern side of Scapa Flow, and harbour routines were adopted which allowed leave ashore. This meant visiting the town of Kirkwall with its pubs, fishing trips, picnics, swimming and hillwalking. In winter, though, these things were usually all but impossible. In winter, Orkney was not a place for the faint of heart.

In late 1914, while the defences of Scapa Flow were being improved, Jellicoe sent the pre-dreadnoughts of the 3rd Battle Squadron south to the Firth of Forth, accompanied by the armoured cruisers of the 3rd Cruiser Squadron, supported by half a flotilla of destroyers. These largely obsolete warships were of little use to Jellicoe, and in a largely unprotected Scapa Flow they became a liability. This preceded the moving of the pre-dreadnoughts even further south in mid-1915, to bolster the defences of the Channel Fleet, and the forces covering the Straits of Dover. The advantage of the Firth of Forth was that it was relatively easy to protect using a combination of minefields and shore defences. Conversely, it was also relatively easy to block, by German-laid mines. So, a strong minesweeping force was maintained there, in the naval base at Rosyth.

Rosyth Dockyard was an extremely useful asset for the Royal Navy. Work on it began in 1903, as the possibility of a naval war with Germany first materialized.

THE GRAND FLEET LYING AT ANCHOR IN SCAPA FLOW, AUGUST 1915 (overleaf)

When the war began, the Grand Fleet's anchorage in Scapa Flow in Orkney was undefended. However, after several months of work, building gun batteries, stringing booms across the entrances, blocking other smaller channels and laying minefields, it was considered fully defensible. From then until the end of the war, Scapa Flow provided a secure base for the fleet. Scapa Flow was well-placed to launch sorties into the northern portion of the North Sea. However, despite the fleet's frequent sweeps, the enemy proved elusive. Consequently, the crews spent long months in idleness, with little to occupy them apart from ship maintenance, training and occasional trips ashore for recreation.

This illustration shows part of the main fleet anchorage to the north of the island of Flotta. Lying at anchor there is the 2nd Battle Squadron, a third of the British battlefleet. The dreadnoughts are anchored three cables (or 600yds) apart from each other, in lines made up of their divisions. In the foreground is HMS *King George V* (with HMS *Ajax*, HMS *Centurion* and HMS *Erin* in line astern of her), while anchored in another line off their port side is the squadron's second division, made up of the Orion-class dreadnoughts HMS *Orion*, HMS *Monarch*, HMS *Conqueror* and HMS *Thunderer*. Lying beyond them is the light cruiser *Boadicea*. The flag at the forepeak of *King George V* denotes this is the flagship of Vice-Admiral Geroge Warrender, the squadron commander.

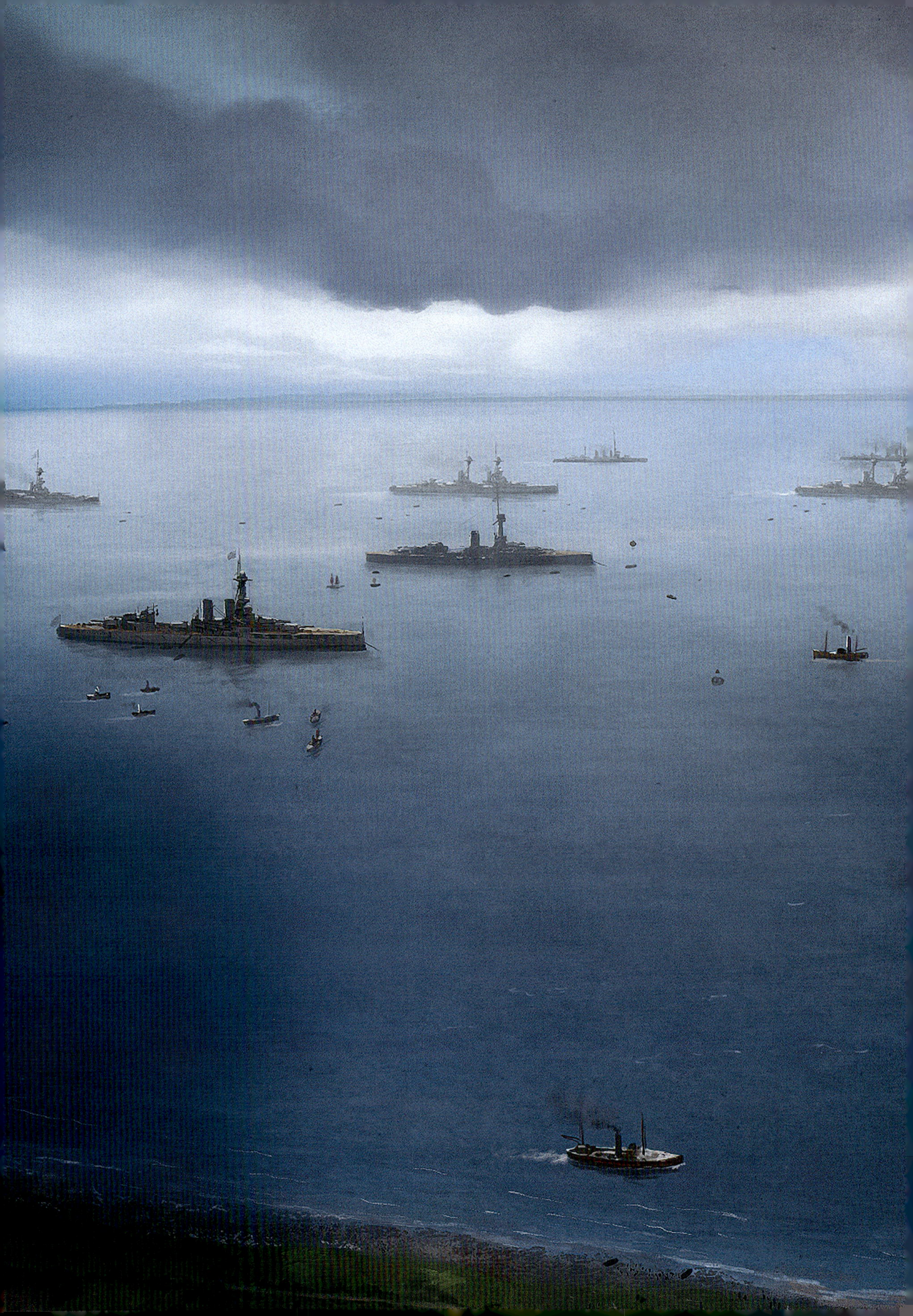

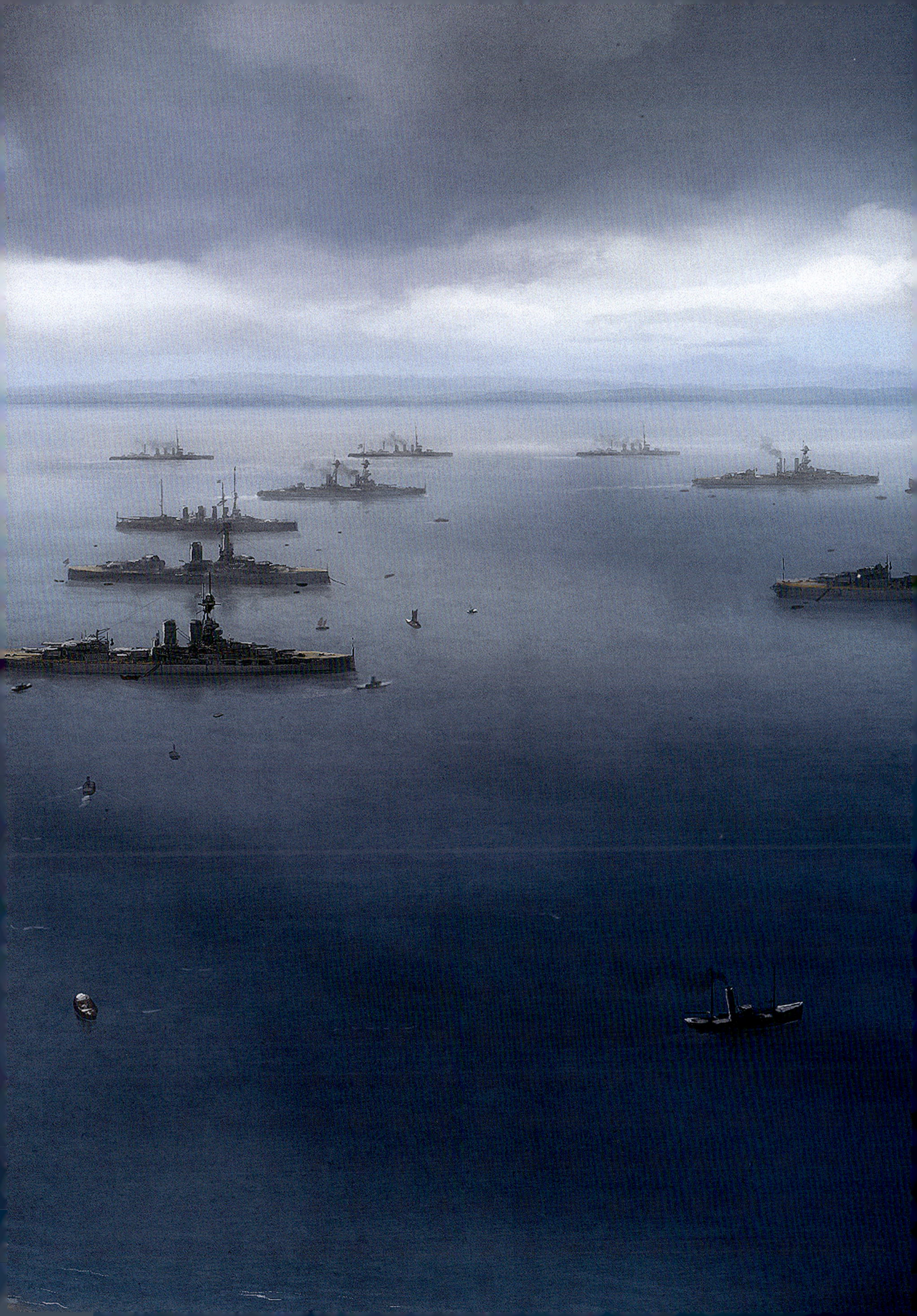

The site itself covered over a thousand acres, and included berthing for up to 22 pre-dreadnought battleships inside a protected basin. The base's main feature though, was its dry dock. While a small floating dry dock in Scapa Flow was available for the maintenance and repair of destroyers or light cruisers, it was too small to be of any use for larger warships. In early 1916 the dry dock in Rosyth was completed, and its first guest that March was the pre-dreadnought battleship HMS *Zealandia* of the 3rd Battle Squadron. Less than three months later, after Jutland, it would be used to assist the repair of several of the fleet's battlecruisers.

By then, Rosyth had become the base for Vice-Admiral Beatty's Battlecruiser Squadron. This was a result of the German raid on Scarborough, Hartlepool and Whitby on 16 December 1914. In the eyes of the Admiralty, it took the Grand Fleet too long to respond, as the steaming time from Scapa Flow was over 12 hours. In response to public criticism, the First Sea Lord made the decision to relocate the battlecruisers to Rosyth. Jellicoe's opposition to this was overruled, while Beatty was delighted to be more autonomous, as well as closer to the social delights of Edinburgh. However, he had reservations about the risk of his fleet being 'mined in' there. Still, on 20 December 1914, Beatty's battlecruisers, accompanied by Goodenough's 1st Light Cruiser Squadron, were sent to Rosyth, which would become their permanent base for the remainder of the war. Their anchorage though, was in the Firth of Forth itself, between the base and the Forth Rail Bridge.

This was all part of a growing feeling in the Admiralty that Scapa Flow was too remote. Jellicoe disliked the Firth of Forth and Cromarty Firth as anchorages

A view of the Grand Fleet at anchor in Scapa Flow in December 1917. The battlefleet lies in the main anchorage, nearest the viewpoint on the island of Flotta, while smaller warships in the background are anchored off the Orkney mainland, near Houton. (oil painting by Sir John Lavery)

for the same reason they had been ruled out before the war – they were too easy to block by enemy-laid mines. Jellicoe also felt both locations were far more prone to mist and fog than Scapa Flow, so much preferred the maintenance of his fleet base in Orkney. Both Churchill and Fisher favoured the partial use of the two southern anchorages, especially after the German raids on the English coast in late 1914 and the Dogger Bank action of the following January. As Fisher put it in a letter to Jellicoe in April 1915: 'The fundamental fact is that you can never be in time as long as you are at Scapa Flow, and therefore there will never be a battle with the German High Seas Fleet unless von Pohl goes north especially to fight you – and that he will never do!' Admiral von Pohl, who assumed command of the High Seas Fleet in early February 1915, was considerably more cautious than his predecessor, Admiral von Ingenohl, or his successor, Vizeadmiral von Scheer.

Jellicoe countered, with Beatty's support, that the battlecruisers should be moved north to the Cromarty Firth, while the battlefleet remain in Scapa Flow, as nowhere else could accommodate them. He also pointed out that it took longer to leave the Firth of Forth due to tides than it did from Scapa Flow. The Admiralty ignored this, and after Beatty's command was formally redesignated the Battlecruiser Fleet in February 1915, his command remained in the Firth of Forth.

The Cromarty Firth, a dozen miles north of Inverness, had a narrow entrance, just over two-thirds of a nautical mile wide, but once inside it stretched for 12 miles, with the area between Cromarty and Invergordon providing a useful and secure deep-water anchorage. By August 1914, it was designated a second-class base, but at that point it lacked adequate defences. However, it was a simple enough business to protect this narrow entrance with booms and coastal defences, and by late October the anchorage there was deemed 'reasonably secure'. By early 1915, an induction loop was added to detect U-boats attempting to sneak inside the sea loch. By the start of the war, a small logistical and dockyard repair base had been established at the small town of Invergordon, with jetties, oil tanks and coal yards, workshops and railway facilities.

In early 1915, against Jellicoe's wishes, and again in response to the Scarborough raid, Vice-Admiral Warrender's 2nd Battle Squadron was moved to the Cromarty Firth, where it would more speedily be able to support Beatty's battlecruisers in the event of another German sortie into the central North Sea. In the Dogger Bank operation of January 1915, it was therefore the only element of the battlefleet which was close enough to play a minor part in the British response to the German sortie, before the High Seas Fleet withdrew back to Wilhelmshaven. So, from early 1915 on, Jellicoe's Grand Fleet were scattered between three different anchorages. Scapa Flow though, remained the administrative, logistical and operational base of the fleet for the remainder of the war.

COMBAT AND ANALYSIS

THE FLEET IN COMBAT

The general stereotype of the Grand Fleet is that its hugely expensive dreadnoughts spent much of the war swinging at anchor in Scapa Flow, and rarely put to sea. When it did venture out, to fight the German High Seas Fleet at Jutland on 31 May 1916, the clash was indecisive, but it was the British who had the worst of the encounter. This is a wildly inaccurate summary of the Grand Fleet's performance during the war, and it still persists to this day, based on a combination of British public anger at not being handed the naval victory they craved, and German propaganda, concentrating on the losses in men and ships, rather than the strategic picture. In reality, Admiral Jellicoe's Grand Fleet not only emerged the clear winners at Jutland, but throughout the war they regularly put to sea, in the hope of drawing their opponents into battle.

The Long Wait

The Grand Fleet conducted its first sweep of the North Sea on the day war was declared, heading into the Norwegian Sea to support the work of the Northern Patrol. After returning to refuel in Scapa Flow, it put to sea again on 8 August to patrol the area between Orkney and Stavanger in southern Norway. Jellicoe returned to Scapa Flow two days later, leaving the battlefleet to continue its sweep, looking for German cruisers or merchantmen attempting to make it home before the blockade was fully established. Jellicoe's return to Scapa Flow was so he could communicate with the Admiralty using his land wire link, which reveals the inadequate degree of wireless communications available to the Grand Fleet at the start of the war. Afterwards, he rejoined the fleet and resumed the sweep until it returned to Scapa Flow on 13 August.

This was the first of numerous sweeps conducted by the Grand Fleet during the opening months of the war. This was in part because Jellicoe didn't consider Scapa Flow a secure base. He had already requested that the Admiralty establish a coaling base at Loch Ewe, on the west coast of the Scottish Highlands, beyond the reach of prowling U-boats. However, it also allowed Jellicoe to practise fleet manoeuvres and gunnery. In Jellicoe's eyes, it was vital that this was conducted regularly, to weld the fleet together and increase its standards of professionalism. This continued until the winter, with the fleet tending to coal at Loch Ewe rather than Scapa Flow.

The Grand Fleet as a complete entity wasn't involved in the first real naval clash of the campaign, the battle of Heligoland Bight on 28 August 1914. It came about because of a British plan to use light forces – cruisers and destroyers – to raid the German patrols operating in the Heligoland Bight. This involved both Beatty's battlecruisers and Commodore Goodenough's 1st Light Cruiser Squadron, who provided distant support for the attacking force. In the closing stages of this scrappy engagement, both formations managed to join in the fight and acquitted themselves well. In fact, Beatty's battlecruisers allowed the British light forces to extricate themselves, before superior numbers of German cruisers could engage them.

This though, wasn't really the Grand Fleet's fight. Instead, Jellicoe saw his task as supporting the Northern Blockade, and conducting sweeps of the North Sea, to draw out the enemy, or to encounter him if the Germans conducted a sweep of their own. The next significant sweep in late September is worth mentioning here, as it established the Grand Fleet's willingness to engage the enemy and demonstrated the Germans' lack of enthusiasm to accept the challenge, unless the odds were more favourable. On 7 September, the Grand Fleet left Loch Ewe and headed north, to enter the North Sea through the Fair Isle Channel. It then steamed to the south-east, on a direct course towards the Heligoland Bight. By 12 September it was 110 miles from Wilhelmshaven, the equivalent of just over five hours of steaming. Meanwhile the Harwich Force, supported by Beatty and Goodenough, cruised off the Heligoland Bight, to draw the Germans out.

However, the Germans refused to be drawn, and when thick weather descended, Jellicoe abandoned the operation. Instead, he led the fleet in a sweep of the North Sea, on his way back to Scapa Flow, taking Beatty's forces under his wing as he did so. This sweep was fairly typical of those conducted by the Grand Fleet during the war, and if circumstances had been different, and the High Seas Fleet had put to sea to pursue Beatty, then the major test between the two fleets could have taken place almost two years earlier. What is particularly interesting here is that the components of the deployment used by Jellicoe and Beatty before Jutland were used here. Beatty and the Harwich Force were the

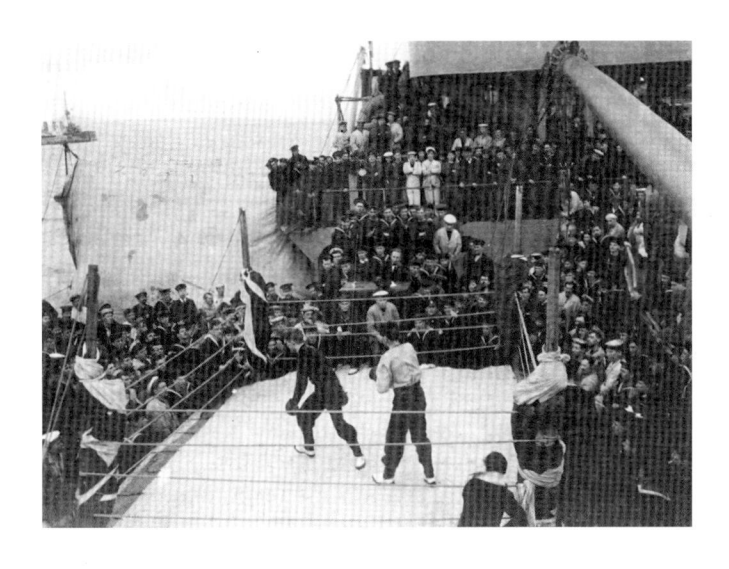

While in Scapa Flow, the crews of the warships of the Grand Fleet often had to make their own entertainment. Here, a boxing match is being held aboard the fleet flagship, HMS *Iron Duke*. There were also limited sports facilities ashore, on the island of Flotta and at the naval base at Lyness in Hoy.

At the outbreak of the war the King George V-class dreadnought HMS *Audacious* joined the 2nd Battle Squadron of the Grand Fleet. However, on 27 October 1914, while conducting squadron exercises off Donegal, *Audacious* struck a mine, and it proved impossible to save the ship. That evening, the crew abandoned ship and the dreadnought sank at 2045hrs, 12 hours after hitting the mine.

bait, with the intention of drawing them northward, onto the guns of Jellicoe's battlefleet. It also demonstrated that even as early as September 1914, the Grand Fleet was actively seeking ways to bring the enemy to battle. This displays a level of confidence by Jellicoe in his ability to defeat his German opponents.

When a clash between the two battlefleets never materialized, Jellicoe did what he could to keep his fleet in readiness for a naval clash if it happened. This took a toll on the fleet, and several ships required repairs and refitting in Portsmouth or Plymouth. Jellicoe wrote that this 'led to two, or three, or even more battleships being absent at a time, on passage, laid up, or refitting. At the German selected moment, our main battlefleet might well at this period have been reduced to 18 ships (all dreadnoughts), whilst the High Sea Fleet was just rising to a strength of 16 dreadnoughts and 16 pre-dreadnoughts.' In other words, if the long-awaited clash came at that point in the war, the British would have temporarily lost their edge in numbers. Indeed, the German Scouting Groups sortied in early November, and the German battlecruisers bombarded Yarmouth on 3 November. Although this was too far away for the Grand Fleet to intervene, Beatty was ordered to prevent the German escape. However, the raid was over before he could intercept them.

This was repeated on 16 December, when the same German force bombarded Hartlepool, Whitby and Scarborough. Forewarned, the Admiralty had already ordered Jellicoe to send Beatty's battlecruisers and Warrender's 2nd Battle Squadron to intercept the raiders, supported by Goodenough's light cruisers and Packenham's armoured cruisers. The destroyers of the Harwich Force also headed north to intervene. Jellicoe ordered Beatty to move to a position to the north-east of Dogger Bank, to intercept Vizeadmiral Hipper's battlecruisers as they withdrew. Jellicoe was aware though, that the German battlefleet would invariably be at sea, to support Hipper's withdrawal, and argued that Beatty lacked the strength to take it on. In the end, Hipper escaped, and a major clash never developed. In a way, Beatty had been lucky, as Admiral von Ingenohl's battlefleet was nearby.

This though, led to the Admiralty insisting that Beatty's command be stationed in the Firth of Forth, and that a powerful battlecruiser squadron be based on the Cromarty Firth, to support it. Both of these moves were made without Jellicoe's approval, and he felt it weakened the fleet. It also led to an argument between

Jellicoe and Fisher over the deployment of the Grand Fleet in Scapa Flow, where it would be hard-pressed to intervene in a German sortie in the central North Sea. The relocation of the battlecruisers – soon to become the Battlecruiser Fleet – and the 2nd Battle Squadron were therefore something of a compromise.

A little over a month after the Scarborough raid, in January 1915, Beatty had another chance to act. The NID's Room 40 had advance warning of a further German battlecruiser sortie, so Beatty and Goodenough were ordered to sea from Rosyth. Beatty would then rendezvous with the Harwich Force off Dogger Bank, before hunting for the enemy. This time, on 24 January, Beatty caught up with Hipper, and in the action which followed, the German armoured cruiser *Blücher* was sunk, although both Beatty and Hipper's battlecruisers suffered damage in the fight as well. Ultimately though, Beatty had let Hipper slip away, and so strategically the battle was indecisive. Jellicoe had followed Beatty, but had been too far away to intervene before the Germans withdrew.

All this time, Jellicoe had been trying to maintain the integrity of the Grand Fleet, and throughout 1915 and early 1916 he conducted joint exercises and sweeps with the detached forces in the Cromarty Firth and the Firth of Forth. The fleet was strengthened too, with new battleships, including the first of the Queen Elizabeth and Royal Sovereign classes, with their 15in. guns. As it was now clear that the Grand Fleet had overtaken its German rivals in terms of strength, Jellicoe was eager to bring about a battle which would establish his fleet's dominance in the North Sea. However, he was also more than happy that the Northern Blockade was still in place and that the economic stranglehold on Germany was really starting to bite.

Much of this period was spent trying to entice the Germans into a fight. However, the new German fleet commander, Admiral von Pohl, was extremely reluctant to place his fleet in harm's way. Undeterred, the Grand Fleet conducted regular sweeps across the North Sea, and while these didn't result in any contact with the enemy, Jellicoe used the opportunity to hone his captains' skills in fleet manoeuvres, as well as his crews in gunnery practice. Jellicoe knew that while the Heligoland Bight was protected by thick belts of mines, the Germans had two exits from it. One lay to the west, past the line of the Frisian Islands, towards Dogger Bank and the Humber. This was effectively beyond the reach of the

The end of the battlecruiser HMS *Invincible* at Jutland. The flagship of Rear Admiral Hood's 3rd Battlecruiser Squadron blew up at 1830hrs while engaging two German battlecruisers. She broke in two, but her bow and stern remained above the water, visible to the British battlefleet as they passed her remains a few minutes later.

Grand Fleet in Scapa Flow, although as seen, a German sortie in this direction could be covered by Beatty's Battlecruiser Fleet, and by the Harwich Force.

The Germans' second route into the North Sea lay to the north, towards Horns Reef and the western seaboard of Denmark. A sortie in this direction was well within range of Scapa Flow, and so, after a rendezvous with his detached forces to the south, Jellicoe could head east, to cut the enemy's line of retreat to Wilhelmshaven. In fact in early May 1916, the Grand Fleet carried out a sweep which reached as far east as Horns Reef, with Beatty scouting ahead of the battlefleet almost within sight of the Danish coast. However, the new German fleet commander, Vizeadmiral von Scheer, refused to be drawn, and remained resolutely in port. This kind of German sortie though, was Jellicoe's dearest wish, and was what he had his fleet prepare for during what became known as 'The Long Wait'. A few weeks later, at the end of May, Jellicoe finally had his wish. Intelligence reports confirmed that Scheer was planning to put to sea, and would be heading north.

THE DEPLOYMENT OF THE GRAND FLEET AT SEA, 1915–16

Given the sheer number and variety of warships in the Grand Fleet, Admiral Jellicoe developed well thought-out plans for the fleet's deployment. This diagram shows the Grand Fleet's deployment, outlined in Jellicoe's Battle Order of December 1915. It was assumed that by this stage of a sortie, the Grand Fleet would have combined, with the elements from Scapa Flow, the Cromarty Firth and Firth of Forth, all successfully rendezvousing at sea. The provisional rendezvous point laid down that December was a point 100 nautical miles due east of the Naze, the southernmost tip of Norway, and 230 miles from Scapa Flow. This was designed to intercept a German sortie towards the north, targeting shipping in the Skaggerak. The basic fleet formation would remain the same if the High Seas Fleet was heading towards the British coast. In that case, the primary threat would be to port of the British battlefleet, rather than to starboard, so the leading elements of Vice-Admiral Beatty's Battlecruiser Fleet would be redeployed accordingly.

The intention was that first contact would be made by the light cruiser squadrons attached to Beatty's command. Then the battlecruiser squadrons would intervene. It was likely that the German advance would be spearheaded by their own battlecruiser force, as part of the High Seas Fleet's Scouting Groups. Also supporting Beatty would be the fast battleships of the 5th Battle Squadron, whose firepower could well tip the balance in a clash with Vizeadmiral Hipper's German battlecruisers. While the outcome of this encounter was being decided, Beatty would be supported by attached destroyer flotillas. His primary task, though, was to locate the German battlefleet, and then to draw them away towards the north-west, onto the guns of Jellicoe's dreadnoughts.

Following behind the battlefleet, echeloned to the side closest to the primary threat – the direction the Germans were expected to appear from – were the fleet's armoured cruiser squadrons, supported by other light units. Their task was to prevent any attempt to outflank Jellicoe's columns of dreadnoughts by enemy torpedo boats or destroyers. After all, Jellicoe's most important task, apart from destroying the enemy, was to prevent undue losses to his battlefleet. This fleet deployment, as the Grand Fleet sought to give battle to its German counterparts, was an amalgam – part offensive, part defensive, and yet designed, through good radio communications, to allow Jellicoe to place the battlefleet in the most advantageous position possible when the two dreadnought forces finally entered the fray. This, essentially, is what happened when the long-anticipated clash finally took place at Jutland on 31 May 1916.

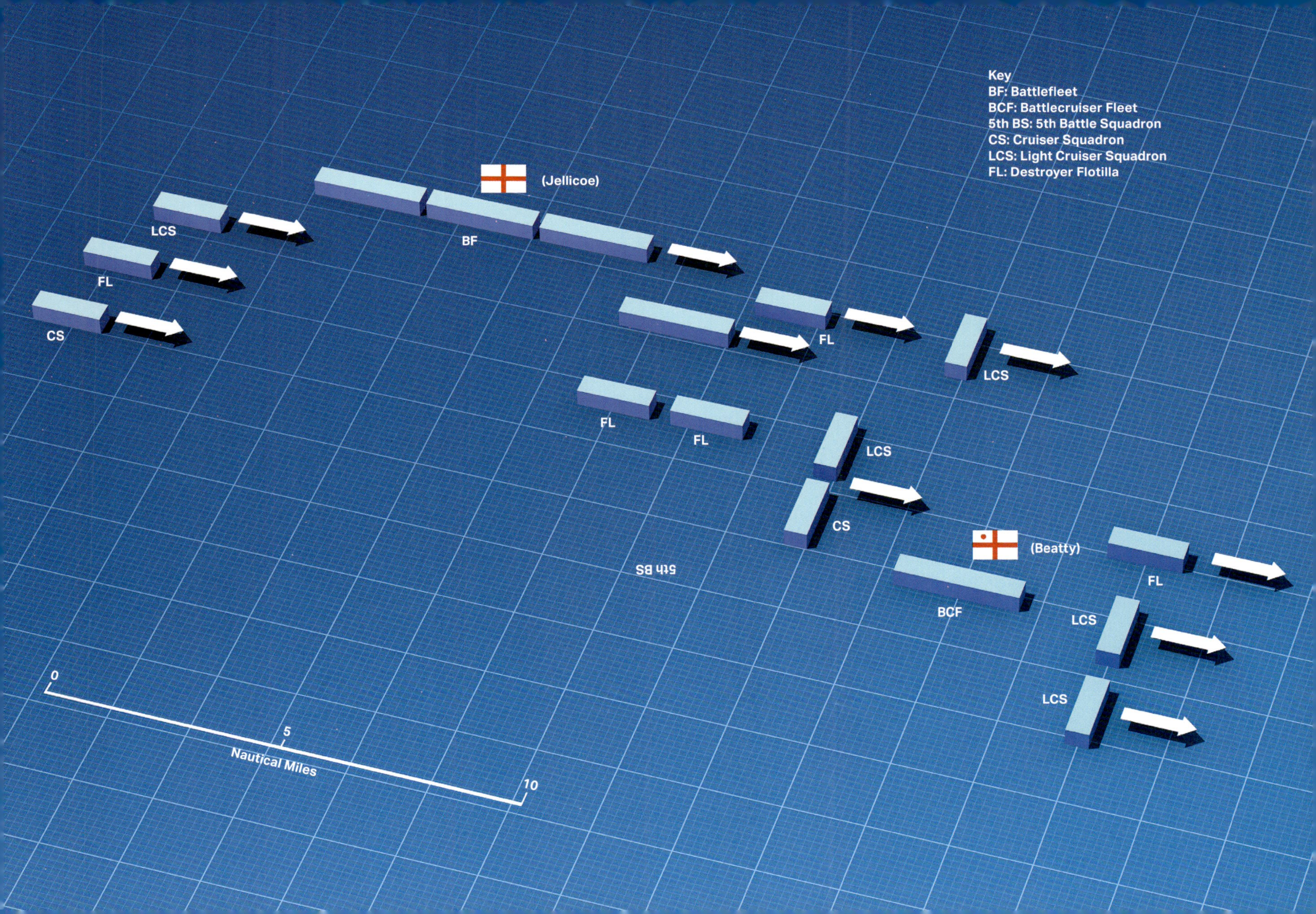
Key
BF: Battlefleet
BCF: Battlecruiser Fleet
5th BS: 5th Battle Squadron
CS: Cruiser Squadron
LCS: Light Cruiser Squadron
FL: Destroyer Flotilla
(Jellicoe)
LCS
FL
CS
BF
FL
LCS
FL
FL
LCS
CS
(Beatty)
FL
BCF
LCS
LCS
5th BS
0
5
10
Nautical Miles

Jutland

Much has been written about the battle of Jutland, including accounts describing every shell hit and the damage it caused. Few naval battles in history have such an extensive historiography. The aim here though, is to concentrate on the battle from the British perspective, concentrating where possible on the viewpoint of the Commander-in-Chief of the Grand Fleet, and the performance of his battlefleet. This, after all, was its real moment of glory, and when it came within an ace of wining the war at sea – or losing it in an afternoon.

On 30 May 1916, the bulk of the Grand Fleet put to sea from Scapa Flow on one of its periodic sweeps of the North Sea. Intelligence reports suggested that the High Seas Fleet might be attempting a sortie towards the Skagerrak, and Jellicoe wanted to be on hand if this turned out to be true. The Battlecruiser Fleet, with the 5th Battle Squadron attached, was ordered to sail from the Firth of Forth, while the 2nd Battle Squadron was also under orders to leave the Cromarty Firth. Jellicoe and Beatty would rendezvous in the North Sea off Jutland at around 1430hrs the following day, 31 May, before continuing eastwards in a sweep towards the Danish coast. Jerram's 2nd Battle Squadron joined the rest of the battlefleet at 1115hrs that morning. Jellicoe then headed off in search of Beatty and the Germans.

However, the rendezvous never took place – at least not as planned. At 1420hrs that afternoon, Beatty's light cruiser screen made contact with a body of German cruisers. The biggest naval clash of the war then came about almost by accident, as at the time Beatty's Battlecruiser Fleet and Hipper's German Scouting Groups were both on roughly parallel courses, out of sight of each other. The German cruiser screen spotted a lone Danish steamer to the west, and the light cruiser *Elbing* was sent to investigate, supported by two torpedo boats. Further to the west, the eastern wing of Beatty's force was scouting ahead of the battlecruiser squadrons, but two light cruisers, *Galatea* and *Phaeton* of the 1st LCS, were sent to investigate the funnel smoke seen to the east. The two sides spotted each other, and *Galatea* duly reported the contact, while hoisting

The Town-class cruiser HMS *Chester* was typical of the light cruisers in the Grand Fleet – sleek, fast and fairly well-armed. At Jutland, though, *Chester* was badly mauled by the German 2nd Scouting Group. One of the fatalities on board was 16-year-old Boy Seaman 'Jack' Cornwall, who earned a posthumous Victoria Cross for staying at his post when the rest of his gun crew were killed or mortally wounded. He too died of his wounds after the battle.

the age-old flag signal 'Enemy in Sight'. Eight minutes later, at 1428hrs, the British cruisers opened fire and the battle of Jutland began.

Both Commodore Alexander-Sinclair of the 1st LCS and Konteradmiral Bödicker of the II Scouting Group requested support from their battlecruisers, and both Beatty and Hipper duly turned towards their enemy. At that moment they were the only capital ships in the area – Jellicoe and the battlefleet was 60 miles to the north, heading towards the south-east, while Scheer's battlefleet was roughly the same distance to the south-east of Hipper. So, it would take roughly three hours for the main battle to begin. In the meantime, both Beatty and Hipper were determined to make their mark. By 1540hrs, the rival battlecruisers could see each other, and Hipper turned onto a parallel course to the British line, but with the Germans angled inward slightly, slowly reducing the range. Eight minutes later, both sides opened fire, at a range of around 9 miles.

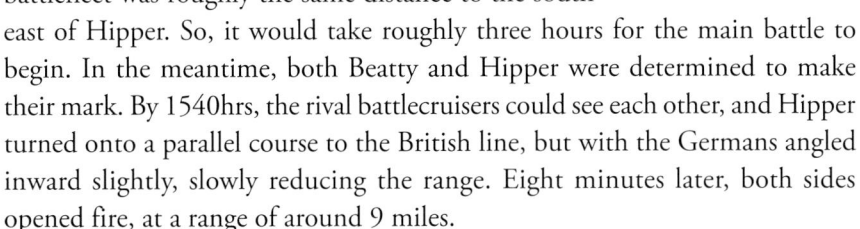

Hipper's five battlecruisers were ranged against Beatty's six, but for some reason Beatty's flagship *Lion* and the *Princess Royal* astern of her both fired on Hipper's flagship *Lützow*, while *Tiger* and *New Zealand*, the fourth and fifth British ships in the line, both fired at *Moltke*, the fourth German ship. This meant that astern of *Lützow*, the *Derfflinger* wasn't fired on at all. The German fire proved far more accurate, and while both sides took hits, it was the British who suffered the most. At 1605hrs, *Indefatigable*, at the rear of the British line, was seen to stagger, and moments later the battlecruiser was ripped apart by an immense explosion. At that moment, over a thousand British sailors lost their lives. The duel continued though, and at 1610hrs the fast battleships of Rear Admiral Evan-Thomas's 5th Battle Squadron joined the fight, concentrating their force on *Moltke* and *Von der Tann* at the rear of the German line.

This, and the damage suffered by the battlecruiser *Seydlitz*, proved enough for Hipper, who turned south, heading directly for the approaching German battlefleet. Beatty turned to follow, and the 'run to the south' began, with both sides still exchanging salvos. Then, at 1626hrs, the battlecruiser *Queen Mary* blew up in an almighty explosion. There were only eight survivors of her crew of more than 1,200 men. Beatty's flagship, *Lion*, would have exploded too when its 'Q' turret was hit, but was saved by the quick thinking of the dying turret commander, Major Harvey RM, who flooded the magazines. It was certainly a disastrous situation for Beatty. Turning to his flag captain, Beatty exclaimed: 'Chatfield, there seems to be something wrong with our bloody ships today.' That was something of an understatement.

The run to the south continued, with first one side then the other launching destroyer or torpedo boat attacks at their opponents. These achieved little though, save for the loss of a few destroyers apiece. Beatty made two major errors

During the 'run to the south' at Jutland, the rival battlecruisers were exchanging fire at a range of about 7½ miles, when at 1626hrs a shell from SMS *Seydlitz* struck HMS *Queen Mary* and the British battlecruiser blew up, disappearing amid a huge column of flame and black smoke which rose a thousand feet into the air. The disaster, seen here from SMS *Moltke*, claimed the lives of 1,266 of *Queen Mary*'s crew.

at this point. First, due to his signalling error, Evan-Thomas wasn't ordered to follow the battlecruisers south, and so his powerful fast battleships lagged behind. Beatty also failed to keep Jellicoe fully appraised of what was happening. In fact, Jellicoe only learned of the loss of *Indefatigable* and *Queen Mary* early the following morning. So, the Commander-in-Chief of the Grand Fleet had to guess what Beatty was doing, and where he was heading. Fortunately, the astute Jellicoe remained on course, which drew his battlefleet closer to Scheer's one, which Jellicoe assumed was out there, somewhere to the south of Hipper.

Sure enough, at 1638hrs, the German battlefleet was sighted. As Beatty ran south, he'd deployed the 2nd LCS ahead of him as a precaution. It was just as well, as lookouts aboard Goodenough's light cruiser, *Southampton*, spotted smoke to the south, and then Scheer's dreadnoughts were spotted. Goodenough immediately warned both Beatty and Jellicoe as he turned his cruisers about. At 1646hrs, when the German dreadnoughts opened fire on *Lion*, Beatty did the same. This meant the British battlecruisers were heading almost directly towards the fast battleships of the 5th Battle Squadron. As they passed, Beatty ordered Evan-Thomas to form a rearguard to cover his withdrawal. Meanwhile, Hipper had turned about as well and was following Beatty from a distance, firing as he went. So, the run to the south turned into a run to the north.

This time, though, it would be the 5th Battle Squadron which would bear the brunt of the fighting. Once again, Beatty's signalling let him down, and it was several minutes before Evan-Thomas was ordered to turn away and follow Beatty to the north. All this time, his battleships were under fire from the German battlefleet. On board the fast battleship *Warspite*, one officer saw the German dreadnoughts clearly, with 'an endless ripple of orange flashes all down the line'. These were the Germans firing the shells which were pounding Evan-Thomas's rearguard. This chase lasted around 30 minutes, with both sides steaming at full speed, some 10 miles apart. With Beatty's battlecruisers now out of sight in the mist and smoke to the north, Evan-Thomas was largely left to his own devices. The British ships were being pounded though, and on Evan-Thomas's flagship, *Barham*, the wireless had been knocked out so he was unable to tell Jellicoe what was happening.

Damage to the battlecruiser HMS *Tiger*, photographed after Jutland, after she put in to Rosyth for repair. *Tiger* was hit 14 times during the battle, and 24 of her crew were killed. The wireless room on the shelter deck was wrecked, but otherwise there was little major damage.

Still, Jellicoe had the gist of it. Scheer's battlefleet was heading north, in pursuit of Beatty and Evan-Thomas, while Hipper's battlecruisers were a little ahead of Scheer, and also in pursuit, to the south-east of Evan-Thomas. The likelihood was that Beatty was trying to draw the Germans northwards, towards the British battlefleet. If everything went well, and he gauged the moment, then he could deploy his dreadnoughts across the path of the enemy. At 1700hrs, Jellicoe signalled the battlefleet, declaring 'Fleet Action Imminent'. In the moment though, thanks to the lack of information, he could only guess where Scheer was in relation to his own dreadnoughts. Just in case, he had already deployed his two cruiser squadrons and single battlecruiser squadron ahead of the battlefleet, in case the Germans were further to the east than he expected.

It was all extremely confusing, and the situation wasn't helped by wireless signals which were clearly inaccurate. It was only at around 1800hrs that things became clearer. Vice-Admiral Burney in *Marlborough*, on being asked by Jellicoe what he could see, reported that Beatty's battlecruisers were to the south-south-west, steering east with *Lion* in the lead. His flagship was on the right of the British formation, and so he had the best view. Behind the battlecruisers, Burney could also see Evan-Thomas's 5th Battle Squadron. This meant that the enemy were drawing close too, and would now be around 20 miles to the south. Somewhere to the south-east then, would be Hipper's battlecruisers. This meant that thanks to the reduced visibility due to all the funnel smoke and mist, Beatty had managed to screen the approach of Jellicoe's battlefleet from both Scheer and Hipper. The crisis point of the battle was fast approaching.

First though, there was an unexpected clash to the south-east. Rear Admiral Hood's 3rd Battlecruiser Squadron, which was several miles ahead of Jellicoe, had turned west, towards the sound of the gunfire. So too did some accompanying light cruisers and destroyers. Unwittingly, this placed them in the path of Hipper's Scouting Groups. At 1730hrs, the light cruiser *Chester* came across a squadron of German cruisers, and in the exchange that followed, was badly damaged. Then *Hood*'s three battlecruisers appeared, and opened fire at a range of 4 miles. The light cruiser *Wiesbaden* was hit and left dead in the water, while the other German cruisers withdrew. Next, the destroyer flotillas of both sides clashed in a furious melee, which cost the British 4th Flotilla a destroyer, the *Shark*.

Then it was the turn of the British 1st Cruiser Squadron, which Rear Admiral Arbuthnot led in a charge towards the German cruisers. They opened fire at 1805hrs, but within ten minutes they came across Hipper's far more powerful

A depiction of the battlecruiser action at the battle of Jutland on 31 May 1916. In the foreground is HMS *Lion*, flagship of Vice-Admiral Beatty. During the battle, *Lion* was hit by 13 12in. shells fired by SMS *Lützow*, and only avoided destruction by the prompt flooding of 'Q' turret's magazine, after the turret was hit and set ablaze. (watercolour by William L. Wyllie)

battlecruisers, which opened up at a range of just 4 miles. Within minutes, Arbuthnot's flagship, the armoured cruiser *Defence*, was blown up, with the loss of all hands, and her sister ship *Warrior* was crippled. It was a foolhardy, needless encounter, but things were about to get much worse. At that point, Beatty spotted Hipper's battlecruisers again and the two sides traded blows. Then, approaching Beatty from the east, Hood's squadron appeared and joined in the fight. Further to the west, the 5th Battle Squadron were also still in action against the steadily advancing German battlefleet. Hipper's battlecruisers turned away from the British, but as they did they hit Hood's flagship, *Invincible*, now 5 miles away to the north-east. At 1833hrs, Hood's flagship was hit again by a shell from *Derfflinger*, and *Invincible* was torn in two, leaving her bow and stern sticking out of the sea.

Strangely though, these distractions might well have played into Jellicoe's hands. By 1800hrs, he was aware that the German battlefleet was approaching from the south, deployed in line ahead. His own battlefleet was advancing in six parallel columns, each made up of a division of four dreadnoughts, with Jerram's 2nd Battle Squadron to port, Sturdee's 4th Battle Squadron in the centre, together with Jellicoe's fleet flagship, *Iron Duke*, and Burney's 1st Battle Squadron making up the two starboard columns. Clearly, Jellicoe had to deploy his battlefleet into line, but it could be done three different ways. These essentially involved turning into line to port, turning to starboard or

JELLICOE'S TRAP, JUTLAND, 31 MAY 1916, 1829HRS

The *raison d'être* of the Grand Fleet was to bring its German counterpart, the High Seas Fleet, to battle and to comprehensively destroy it. Although this never happened, for a few brief minutes during the battle of Jutland it looked as if it might and ensure a victory on the scale of Trafalgar. This diagram shows the afternoon of the 31st May when the two battlecruiser forces clashed, Jellicoe's battlefleet closed with the enemy, guided by the intermittent reports sent to him from Beatty. Sea haze and smoke hid the approaching enemy, but nevertheless, Jellicoe had to make a decision which could, potentially, end the naval war before nightfall. His battlefleet was steaming in six parallel columns. At 1815hrs, he gave the order for them to turn to port so that the entire battlefleet was formed into a single line, with the dreadnought *King George V* at its head. It was exactly the right decision. Ten minutes later, the German battlefleet was sighted to the south, heading directly towards the British dreadnoughts. In naval parlance, the British were 'crossing the T' of the German battlefleet.

At 1829hrs, Jellicoe gave the signal for his dreadnoughts to open fire. The devastating firepower of 14 dreadnought battleships was unleashed, with more dreadnoughts joining in after they completed their turn into line. The range was between 6 and 7 miles. This force was concentrated at the head of the German column, where the leading dreadnought, SMS *König*, was quickly hit. What saved the German battleship was a special manoeuvre, the *Gefechtskehrtwendung* ('Battle turn away') ordered by the German commander, Vizeadmiral Scheer, which had his whole column of dreadnoughts turn simultaneously to starboard, until the column was heading in the opposite direction from the British fleet. Within minutes, the two sides lost contact and the moment had gone. Surprisingly, the same situation repeated itself just over half an hour later, but again the Germans reversed course and thus avoided annihilation. Admiral Jellicoe had done everything right, and his fleet had performed perfectly. Were it not for that unusual German manoeuvre, the High Seas Fleet would have been caught in a trap and destroyed piecemeal.

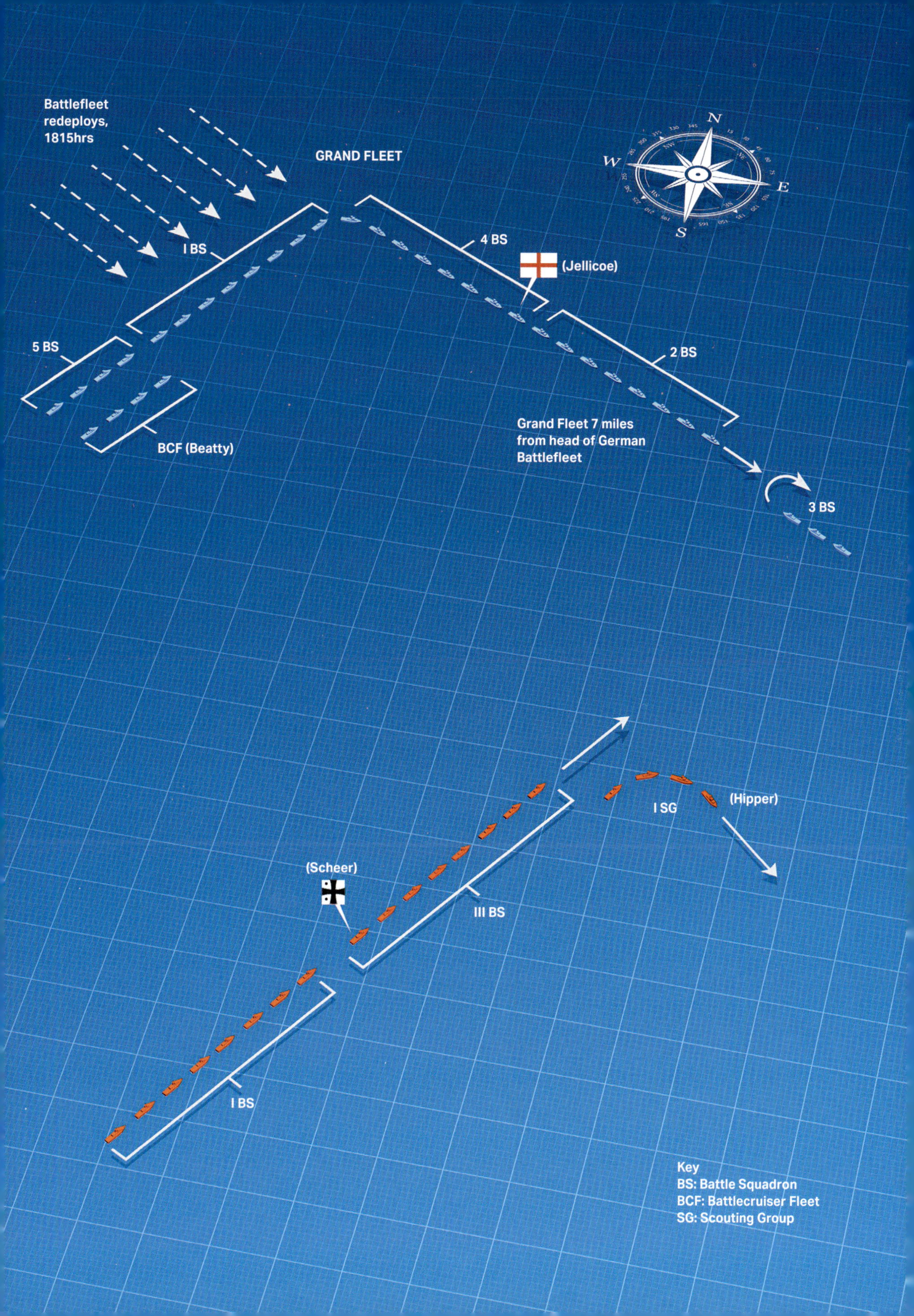

Battlefleet redeploys, 1815hrs
GRAND FLEET
N
E
S
W
I BS
4 BS
(Jellicoe)
5 BS
2 BS
BCF (Beatty)
Grand Fleet 7 miles from head of German Battlefleet
3 BS
I SG
(Hipper)
(Scheer)
III BS
I BS
Key
BS: Battle Squadron
BCF: Battlecruiser Fleet
SG: Scouting Group

forging ahead, with the two flanking squadrons falling into place astern of the 4th Squadron. Making the wrong decision could have a profound effect on the outcome of the battle. In the end, Jellicoe crossed the bridge of *Iron Duke* to the ship's compass, peered into the murk to the south-east, and then gave his order.

At 1814hrs, the long-awaited signals from Beatty and Evan-Thomas had told Jellicoe exactly where Scheer's battlefleet was. At 1815hrs, Jellicoe ordered the signal hoisted which would begin the manoeuvre – a turn in succession to port, to form line of battle on the port column; in other words, behind Jerram. A minute later, the signal was dipped and the battlecruiser fleet began its change of formation from column into line. As soon as it began, Jellicoe ordered Jerram in *King George V*, which was now leading the line, to turn to starboard and steer to the west. The speed of the battlefleet was also reduced to 16 knots. It was a masterly move, which placed the whole of the British battlefleet in line, and steaming across the path of Scheer's approaching dreadnoughts. In naval warfare, 'crossing the T' of the enemy – where all your guns could bear on the opponent, but he could only reply with his leading ship – was the perfect position to be in, at least for the fleet at the top of the 'T'.

So, by 1829hrs, just as the head of Scheer's battlefleet heaved into view, Jellicoe's dreadnoughts were perfectly placed to pour their broadsides into the head of the enemy line. The firing began as soon as the enemy were spotted, and soon shells were falling all around the leading ships of the German line – the dreadnoughts *König, Grosser Kurfürst, Markgraf* and *Kaiser*. This was the moment the Grand Fleet had been waiting for. *Iron Duke* alone fired nine salvos in five minutes – a total of 90 13½in. shells. *König* was seen to stagger under the impact of the hits, while the dreadnoughts astern of her were seen being hit too. The annihilation of the German battlefleet was now a near certainty. However, Jellicoe hadn't reckoned on the German manoeuvre of *Gefechtskehrtwendung* ('Battle turn away').

This was a manoeuvre which was unknown to the British. It involved the simultaneous 16-point turn of the entire battlefleet, so that in effect it would turn around onto a reciprocal course, until it was heading directly away from the British line. Scheer's order was executed at 1833hrs, and the entire line of German dreadnoughts began a simultaneous turn to starboard. The British were taken completely by surprise. Worse, the funnel smoke generated by the turning ships acted like a smokescreen, which quickly hid Scheer's dreadnoughts from the British. By 1845hrs, the two battlefleets had lost contact with each other and Jellicoe's great chance had passed.

In fact, that wasn't Jellicoe's last opportunity to pound the German battlefleet. After contact was broken, he ordered his battlefleet to head towards the south-east, in case Scheer tried to turn away in that direction, towards his base in Wilhelmshaven. To widen the search area, Jellicoe had his battlefleet form into divisions again, this time into an echeloned formation, with *King George V* to the west in the lead. For his part, Scheer turned his fleet around again, using another *Gefechtskehrtwendung* manoeuvre. As Jellicoe predicted, the German commander was trying to move to the east. A little after 1905hrs, the two fleets caught sight of each other, and the British found themselves in another ideal tactical position, 'crossing the T' of the German fleet for the second time. The British dreadnoughts opened fire at a range of 6–8 miles.

Scheer though, extricated himself by performing another *Gefechtskehrtwendung*, covering it with his now badly battered battlecruisers and then sending in his torpedo boats for a massed attack. The German boats launched their torpedoes at long range – around 2–3 miles – and this was spotted by the British. The standard response by a fleet was to 'comb' the torpedo tracks, either by heading towards the threat or away from it. Jellicoe instinctively chose the latter, which meant that most of his dreadnoughts could outrun the torpedoes, which had a limited range. Still, there were several near misses before the British ships successfully evaded the pursuers. Only *Marlborough* was hit, and the damage caused was minimal. This evasive move, though, had led to contact with the German battlefleet being broken for a second time. All the British had to show for the clash was a number of hits to the leading German dreadnoughts, another mauling of Hipper's battlecruisers before they withdrew, and a few destroyers blown out of the water.

However, Jellicoe had now missed his chance to completely crush the High Seas Fleet. For the remainder of the evening the two fleets headed south, with Jellicoe's Grand Fleet blocking Scheer's route home to Wilhelmshaven. The odd clash took place as darkness fell, but for the most part the two fleets remained out of sight of each other. The wily Scheer though, wasn't going to wait meekly for the slaughter that would surely come at dawn. Instead, he ordered his fleet to turn to the north, and judging his moment he led it to the south-east in an attempt to pass behind the British line. Jellicoe had placed his destroyers

JELLICOE SPRINGS HIS TRAP, BATTLE OF JUTLAND, 31 MAY 1916, 1830HRS (overleaf)

Since the war began, during sweeps into the North Sea, Admiral Jellicoe had had his fleet perform manoeuvres until every captain knew exactly what was expected of them. As a result, Jellicoe could rely on them to follow his orders, come what may. Jellicoe had already planned a strategy which revolved around using the battlecruiser fleet to draw the enemy battlefleet onto the guns of his dreadnoughts. At Jutland, despite the lack of clear information, this plan worked to perfection. Almost intuitively, Jellicoe knew when to deploy his battlefleet into line and how to place it across the path of the German dreadnoughts.

This illustration shows the fleet flagship, HMS *Iron Duke*, moments after the battlefleet opened fire on the head of the German line, some 7 miles to the south. Jellicoe's flagship is viewed from HMS *Thunderer*, the last of the eight dreadnoughts of the 2nd Battle Squadron, which formed the line ahead of the flagship. Astern of *Iron Duke* are other dreadnoughts of the 1st Battle Squadron, HMS *Royal Oak*, HMS *Superb*, HMS *Canada* and four more ships astern of them. Even further back, still forming into line, are eight more dreadnoughts of the 3rd Battle Squadron. Together, they could bring an overwhelming weight of fire onto the head of the German battlefleet. A British victory was all but assured until the German ships surprised the British by simultaneously turning away, disappearing in the smoke. Essentially, the trap had been sprung but the Germans managed to wriggle free.

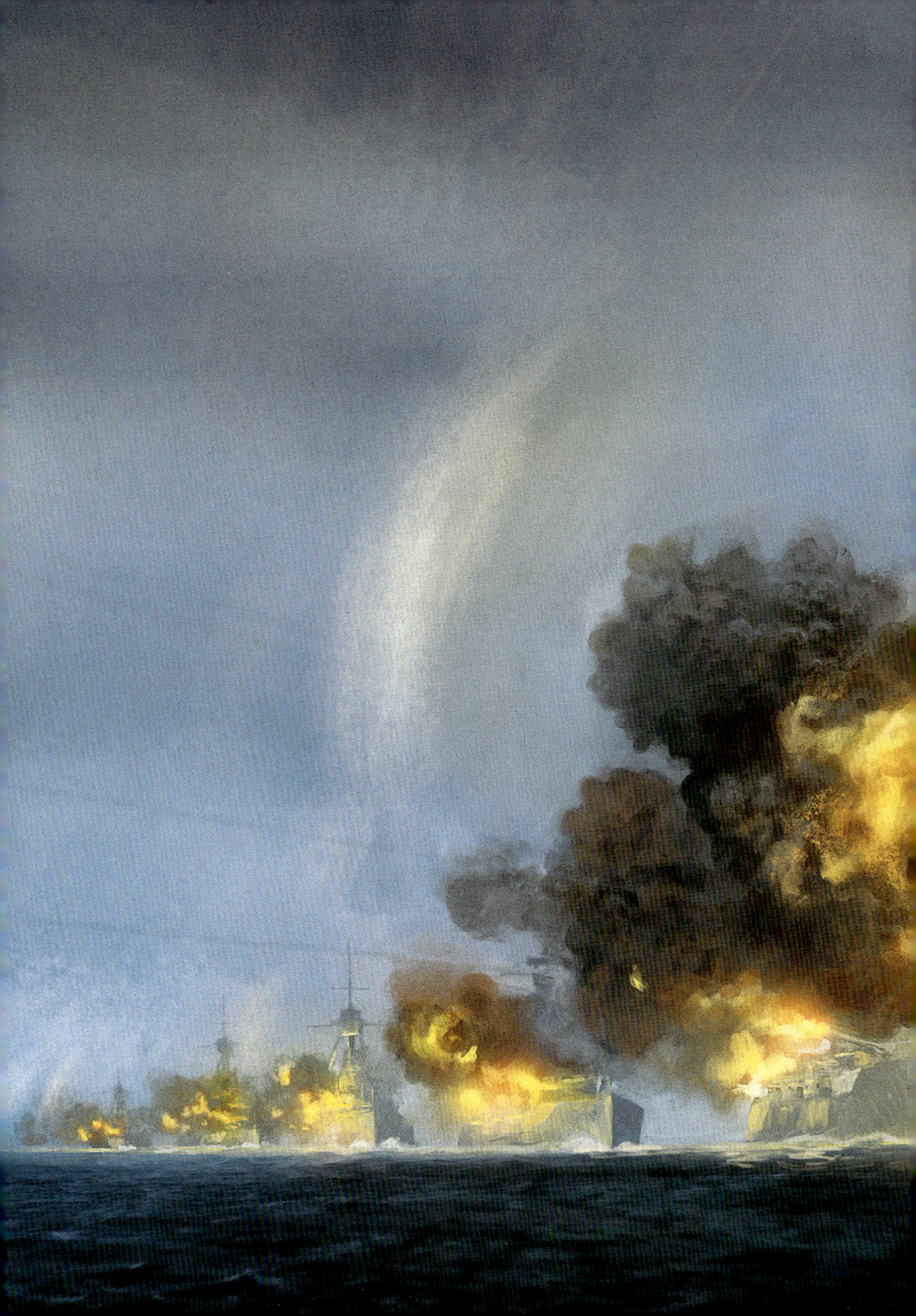

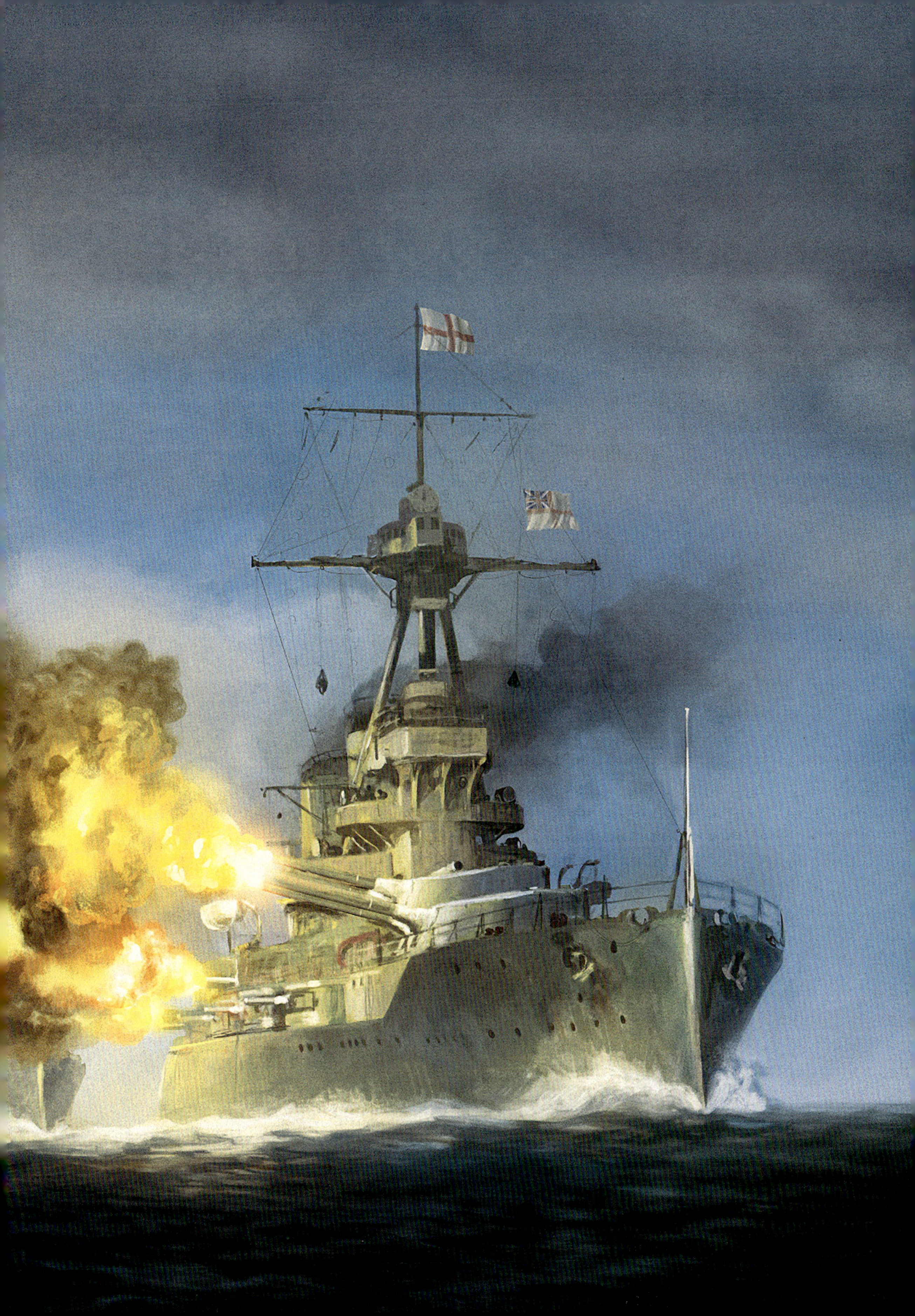

British sailors, wearing their anti-flash hoods, gloves and goggles, leaning on a minesweeping paravane on the deck of their warship, watching the surrender of the German High Seas Fleet on 21 November 1918. The Allies were taking no chances, and so their ships were readied for action, just in case.

there, and the Germans had to fight their way through them. Three cruisers and a pre-dreadnought battleship were lost in the night battle that followed, but Scheer eventually won through, and by 0300hrs, he was clear and his battered fleet was on its way home.

Nobody though, had taken the time to tell Jellicoe what was happening. So as dawn broke, Jellicoe hoped to find the High Seas Fleet to the west of him, and to set about its destruction. Instead, sunrise on 1 June revealed an empty sea. Jellicoe had comprehensively outmanoeuvred and outfought his rival, but that morning he was left with very little to show for it. After the battle, the balance sheet was very much in the Germans' favour. The Grand Fleet had lost three battlecruisers (*Queen Mary*, *Indefatigable* and *Invincible*), three cruisers (*Defence*, *Warrior* and *Black Prince*) and eight destroyers. The German tally was the battlecruiser *Lützow*, which had to be scuttled, the pre-dreadnought battleship *Pommern*, four light cruisers and five destroyers. In all, the British lost 6,094 men in the battle, to 2,551 Germans.

This though wasn't the real story. Yes, the Grand Fleet had failed to annihilate the High Seas Fleet, despite two golden opportunities to do just that. The German propaganda machine made the most of the losses, and the German press proclaimed the 'Battle of Skagerrak' a great German victory. The truth though, was quite the opposite. It was the German fleet which had run for home, leaving the British in control of the sea. The Germans were now aware that the Risk Theory had failed, and that it was now impossible to win a victory at sea over the Grand Fleet. The economic blockade of Germany would now continue, and by mid-1916 it was having a real effect, and food became increasingly scarce. In any tally sheet that counted, it was the Grand Fleet which had emerged victorious from Jutland, and it would continue to control the North Sea battleground until the end of the war. Jutland though, would be the last major clash between the two navies.

The Victory of Seapower

The High Seas Fleet would put to sea again. This time, though, thanks to the damage suffered by the High Seas Fleet – particularly the scouting forces – it was comprehensively outnumbered by the Grand Fleet. Scheer wrote to the kaiser, to tell him that the war wasn't going to be won by a clash of arms at sea. Instead, Scheer declared that only an attack against British trade could lead to victory. In other words, victory lay through unrestricted U-boat warfare. This was unleashed in February 1917, and although British mercantile losses were high, it wasn't enough to ensure victory. Instead, as the economic blockade really bit in, Germans began starving, and war production fell away, thanks to a lack of raw material.

Still, the High Seas Fleet needed to sortie again, if for no other reason than to prove it was still in the fight. So, on 18 August Scheer led a sortie, hoping to resurrect the plan to draw elements of the grand Fleet into battle on heavily advantageous terms. In the end the sortie proved unsuccessful, as thanks to Room 40 the British responded quickly. On the afternoon of 19 August, with Jellicoe, Beatty and Commodore Trywhitt of the Harwich Force closing in, Scheer gave the order to withdraw. Another German sortie in November 1916, to support the recovery of a U-boat, led to the torpedoing of two dreadnoughts, *Grosser Kurfurst* and *Kronprinz*, by a British submarine, J-1. The dreadnoughts were able to limp home to Wilhelmshaven, but it showed that the submarine screen the British had established around the Heligoland Bight was now considerably more of a threat to the Germans than it had been. Consequently, German sorties would now only be made if sufficient anti-submarine escorts were available.

On 24 November, Admiral Jellicoe was contacted by the Admiralty, and was offered the post of First Sea Lord. He agreed, and so two days later he turned command of the battlefleet over to his deputy, Vice-Admiral Sir Cecil Burney, and took his flagship south to Rosyth. There, on 28 November, Jellicoe hauled down his flag. Command of the Grand Fleet was then turned over to newly promoted Admiral Sir David Beatty. According to Scheer, the kaiser was now even less likely to approve a sortie, as he held Beatty would be more aggressive than Jellicoe had been, and so would push harder to bring about another major encounter. With the numerical odds stacked heavily in the Grand Fleet's favour, this was a battle the German battlefleet would be less likely to extricate itself

THE GRAND FLEET ACCEPTS THE GERMAN SURRENDER, 1918 (overleaf)

At 1100hrs on 11 November 1918, the Armistice came into effect, the guns fell silent and the war came to an end. As part of the agreement, the German High Seas Fleet was to leave Wilhelmshaven, cross the North Sea and surrender to the Grand Fleet off the Scottish coast. Then it would be led north to Scapa Flow, where it would be interned until the peace talks were concluded. Ten days later, at 0900hrs on 21 November, the unarmed ships of the German fleet arrived off the Firth of Forth and steamed in line ahead, passing between two lines of Allied ships, whose crews stood ready to open fire on their old enemy if there was any sign of resistance.

This illustration captures the scene that morning, as the first of the German ships passes between the Allied ships.

The German battlecruisers, at the head of the German line, are led by the light cruiser HMS *Cardiff*. Following astern of the cruiser is the battlecruiser SMS *Seydlitz*, followed by the other remaining German battlecruisers, SMS *Moltke*, SMS *Hindenburg*, SMS *Derfflinger* and SMS *Von der Tann*. Further astern of the battlecruisers are the dreadnoughts of the German battlefleet, in line astern, led by the fleet flagship, SMS *Friedrich der Grosse*. This scene, being recorded here by a film crew, was the tangible evidence of the Grand Fleet's victory in the war at sea. For the crew watching this amazing historic event, this was the moment for which they had spent four long years waiting.

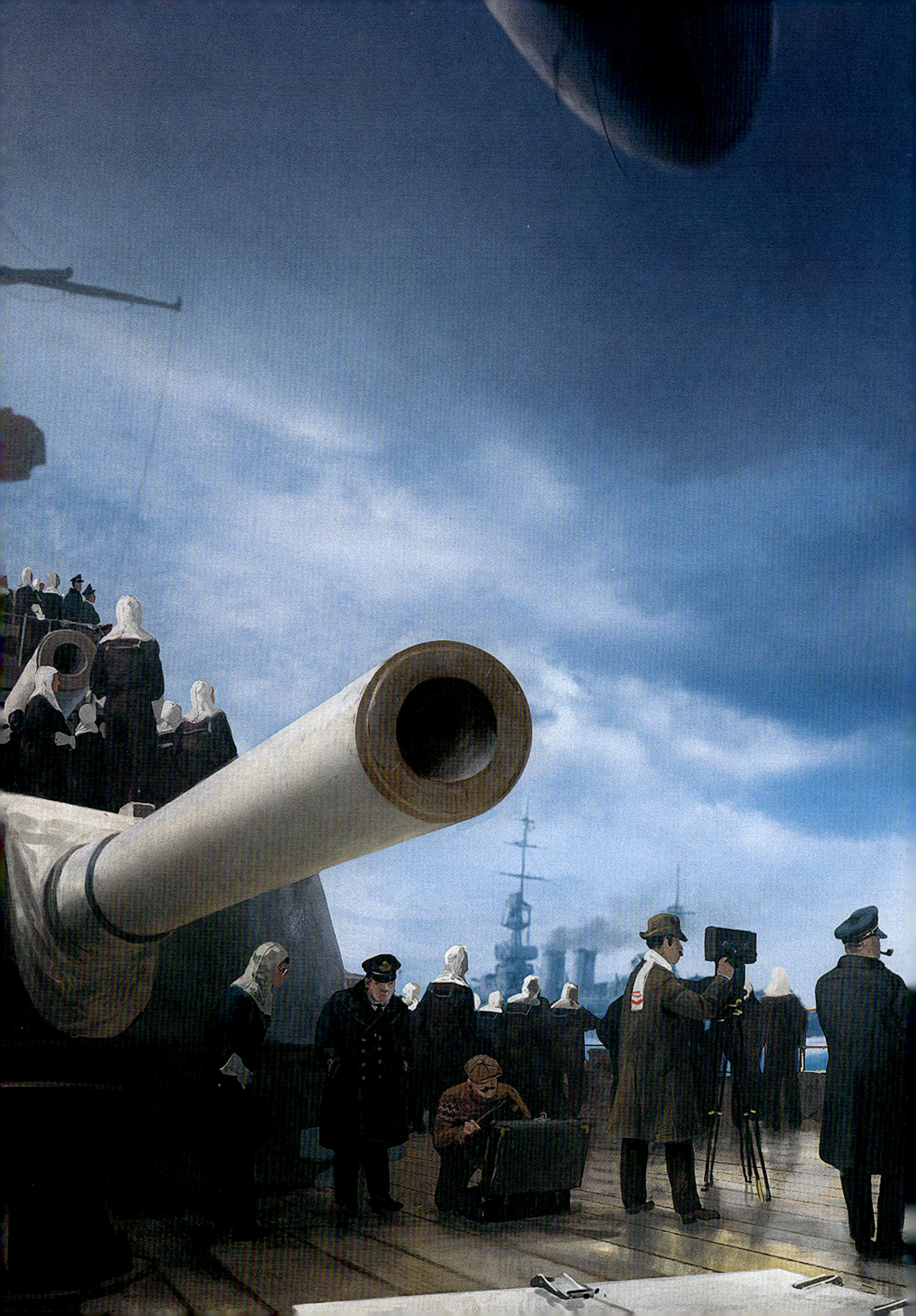

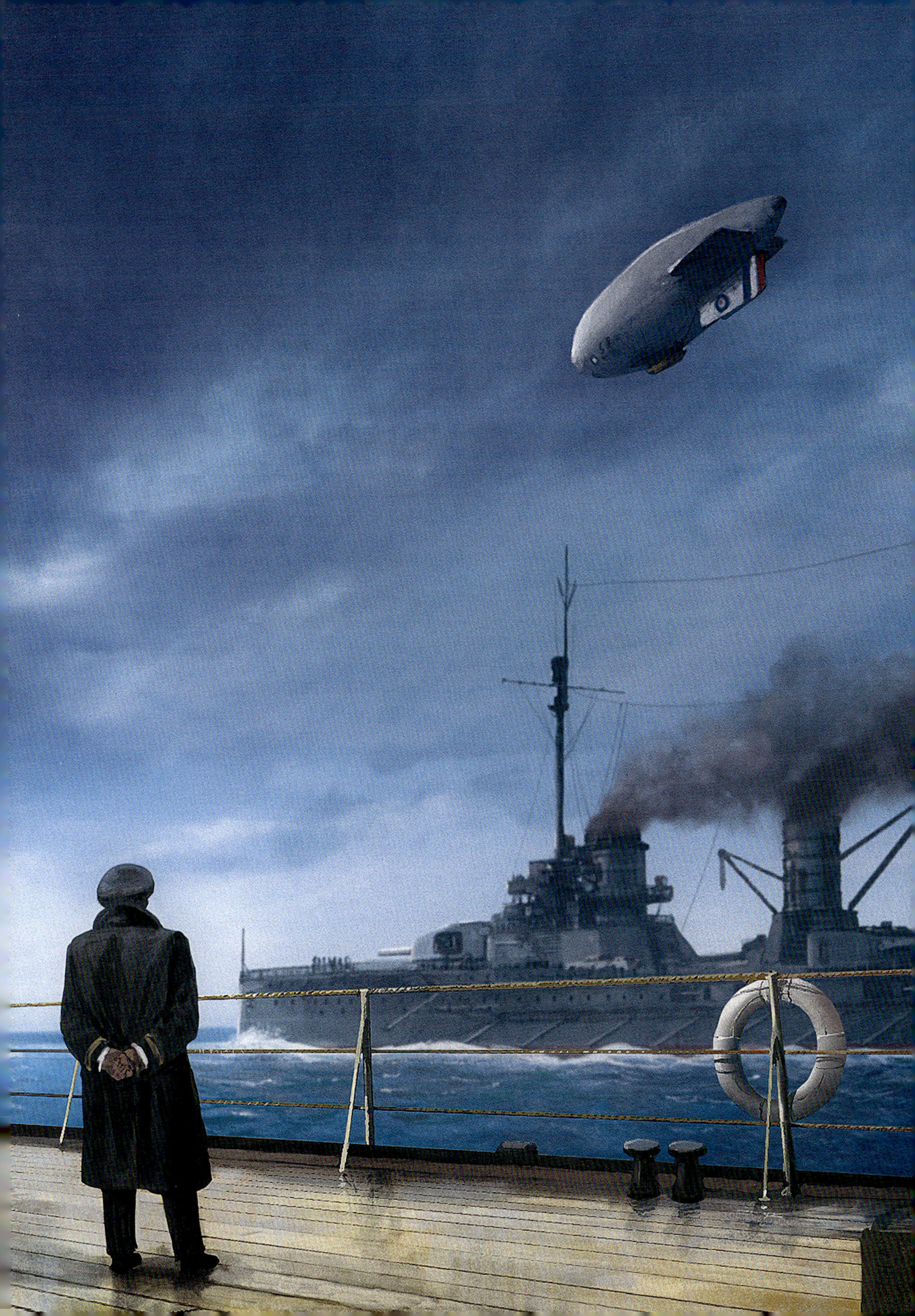

from so neatly. So, the Germans became less inclined to act as aggressively as they had before.

A German sweep of the Skagerrak that December was cancelled due to mechanical problems with *Moltke*, and in early 1917, further sorties were cancelled, or reduced to small torpedo-boat sweeps. A sortie in March was also cancelled, but a cruiser operation in October against a lightly protected convoy proved a limited success. More attacks on convoys were planned but aborted due to bad weather. It was April 1918 before the Germans tried again, and this time *Moltke* was torpedoed by the submarine J-6, and had to be towed home. By then though, Beatty's fleet was closing in, and so Scheer withdrew.

This proved the last sortie by the elements of the High Seas Fleet before the end of hostilities. These though, demonstrated that it still remained a potent force – a 'fleet in being' – but it lacked the strength or even the will to challenge the Grand Fleet in battle. The mutinies of October 1918, which led irrevocably to the German Armistice in early November, finally brought an end to the naval war. The next time the High Seas Fleet put to sea, it was to cross the North Sea to surrender to Admiral Beatty's Grand Fleet, arrayed in all its strength off the Firth of Forth. The Grand Fleet had achieved its purpose: it had prevented the Germans from breaking the blockade of Germany and had exerted its power over the North Sea battleground. The final reward was to receive the surrender of its old enemy, and to escort them to internment on Scapa Flow. Now it was the turn of the Germans lying idly at anchor there to experience the joys of an Orkney winter.

ANALYSIS

The Grand Fleet was created by the will of the British Admiralty on 4 August 1914, the day war was declared. It was made up of the pride of the Royal Navy – the powerful battlefleet of modern dreadnought battleships which would be the arbiters of victory in any naval war. They were hugely expensive, almost prohibitively so, but once Britain and Germany became rivals in a naval arms race, it became politically and militarily impossible to halt the creation of a dreadnought battlefleet. Its creation then, and that of its German rival, the High Seas Fleet, dramatically altered the geopolitical situation in Europe. In the early 20th century, Britain had clear aims. The country was the beating heart of the British Empire, a vast entity that covered a quarter of the world's land mass and held sway over more than 400 million people. The economic power of the empire was immense, but it depended almost entirely on maritime trade. The protection of these vital sea routes lay at the heart of British naval policy. This was the primary task of the Royal Navy, and at the start of the 20th century it had the global muscle to achieve this. For more than two centuries, the Royal Navy was the largest naval force in the world. However, the development of the dreadnoughts threatened to topple Britain from its naval perch. So, it was vital to Britain's global and imperial interests that it built a dreadnought battlefleet, one that was larger than any potential maritime rival. By 1914, this had been achieved, and the Royal Navy possessed the largest and most powerful dreadnought battlefleet in the world.

Finding a purpose for this vast fleet was easy. By 1914, the biggest threat to British global naval primacy and its seaborne trade was the Imperial German Navy. Although Germany had lost the naval arms race – thanks to Britain's larger industrial and shipbuilding might – it still remained a large-enough threat to give Admiral von Tirpitz's Risk Theory a chance of working. To avoid this, the Grand Fleet had to avoid significant losses, while the British government and the Admiralty had to make sure it retained its superiority in numbers. This was achieved with ease during the war – even the battlecruiser losses at Jutland could be absorbed, given the influx of newly commissioned replacements.

So, the High Seas Fleet had to resort to the Mahanian notion of a 'fleet in being', its very existence being sufficient to tie down the bulk of the Grand Fleet, to counter it if it sortied. This too, was achieved successfully – so much so that after Jutland, the German willingness to sortie, and to pursue its 'Force Balancing' stratagem was markedly reduced. In effect, the High Seas Fleet surrendered control of the North Sea battleground to the Grand Fleet.

This had another even more significant result. At the start of the war, Britain imposed a distant blockade of Germany, which prevented the flow of raw materials, food and other vital goods into Germany. As a result, German imports dropped by more than half, and rationing had to be introduced. By the end of 1916 basic staples such as potatoes, meat, wheat and dairy products were in short supply. The German population turned to substitutes such as turnips, but even so there was insufficient produce to go around. By 1917, malnourishment and starvation were widespread, and the situation deteriorated steadily as the war went on. By war's end, it was estimated that at least half a million Germans had died from disease or starvation as a direct result of the blockade. Distasteful though this was, it was the most effective tool available to the Allies to ensure victory.

The Grand Fleet's role in all this was to ensure that the Northern Blockade remained fully effective by preventing any German attempt to break it. This was achieved by discouraging German naval sorties into the northern part of the North Sea. Churchill and Fisher may have been distracted by German sorties against the English coast and insisted on moving some of Jellicoe's fleet further south, so it was better placed to intercept any German sorties there. Jellicoe though, fully understood he was playing a much longer game, and the stationing of the Grand Fleet at Scapa Flow played a key part in it. Only in Scapa Flow could the Grand Fleet guarantee the effective protection of the Northern Blockade. The battle of Jutland was fought as a result of one such northern sortie, in the direction of the blockade line, and it ended with the Germans driven

Some of the ship's company of the destroyer HMS *Swift*, pictured in May 1917, after an action off Dover the previous month. *Swift* formed part of the Grand Fleet's 4th Destroyer Flotilla during 1914 and 1915, after which she was reassigned to the Dover Patrol. Conditions aboard a destroyer were far more cramped than in larger warships, which made long spells isolated in Scapa Flow hard to endure unless the crew found ways to keep themselves entertained.

back into port. So, thanks entirely to the Grand Fleet, the blockade remained in place throughout the war, and would play a major role in forcing Germany's capitulation. Without the Grand Fleet, this would have been impossible.

The battle of Jutland revealed problems with the ships of the Grand Fleet and the way it was operated. As a result, the value of the battlecruiser was seriously questioned. However, the Battlecruiser Fleet remained of value, as its speed – together with the fast battleships – allowed it to intercept German sorties more effectively than the battlefleet. After Jutland though, steps were taken to make the fleet and its ships more effective. Better safety measures were introduced, to reduce the risk of the magazine explosions which caused the loss of three battlecruisers in the battle. Wireless communication procedures were improved, and better equipment fitted, so that the communication problems facing Jellicoe that afternoon weren't repeated. More efficient scouting procedures were developed, and airpower was used to increase the range of these scouting forces, through the use of seaplanes and airships. Jellicoe was never given control of British submarines, but these became more adept at surveillance, operating off the Heligoland Bight, and they were used more aggressively. This in turn served as a deterrent to German sorties beyond their own protective minefields. Just as importantly, in the Grand Fleet itself, gunnery procedures were improved, problems with shells and rangefinding which were brought to light at Jutland were overcome, and professional standards were improved through constant practice. In the end, the Grand Fleet became too powerful for the Germans to contemplate taking it on in another major sea battle. This then, was the way this fleet – the largest force the Royal Navy ever fielded – was instrumental in ensuring victory in the war.

Jellicoe's final words to his men reflected the price he felt in the achievements of the Grand Fleet under his command;

The Iron Duke-class dreadnought HMS Marlborough, manoeuvring at speed astern of another of its class, during exercises in the North Sea in the summer of 1918. By this stage of the war, improved rangefinders were carried, which enhanced gunnery fire control. One of them is visible just behind 'B' turret, immediately below the bridge.

I am convinced that the Fleet gains in efficiency from day to day. We have benefited by experience, and we have turned that experience to good account…. Whilst giving our present foe full credit for high efficiency, I am perfectly confident that in the Grand Fleet they will meet more than their match, ship for ship in all classes, and that the result will never be for one moment in doubt … May your arduous work be crowned with a glorious victory resulting in a just and lasting peace! In November 1918 it was, and all those long years of vigilance and preparedness paid off. The surrender of the High Seas Fleet to the Grand Fleet represented a real display of the effectiveness of seapower – an achievement made possible only by the very existence of this mighty battlefleet, and the men who served in it.

FURTHER READING

Archibald, E. H. H., *The Fighting Ship in the Royal Navy, AD897–1984*, Blandford Press, Poole (1987)
Brown, David K., *The Grand Fleet: Warship Design and Development, 1906–1922*, Seaforth Publishing, Barnsley (1997)
Brown, David K., *Warrior to Dreadnought: Warship Design and Development, 1860–1905*, Seaforth Publishing, Barnsley (2010)
Burt, R. A., *British Battleships of World War 1*, Seaforth Publishing, Barnsley (2012)
Campbell, John, *Jutland: An Analysis of the Fighting*, Conway Maritime Press, London (1986)
Fawcett, H. W. & Hooper, G. W. W., *The Fighting at Jutland*, Chatham Publishing, Jutland (2001)
Friedman, Norman, *Battleship Design and Development, 1905–1945*, Smithmark Publishing, New York (1979)
Friedman, Norman, *Fighting the Great War at Sea: Strategy, Tactics and Technology*, Seaforth Publishing, Barnsley (2014)
Gardiner, Robert (ed), *Conway's All the World's Fighting Ships, 1906–1921*, Conway Maritime Press, London (1985)
Gardiner, Robert, *The Eclipse of the Big Gun: The Warship 1906–45*, Conway Maritime Press, History of the Ship Series, London (1992)
Gordon, Andrew, *The Rules of the Game: Jutland and British Naval Command*, John Murray, London (1996)
Halpern, Paul G., *A Naval History of World War 1*, US Naval Institute Press, Annapolis, MD (1994)
Hodges, Peter, *The Big Gun: Battleship Main Armament, 1860–1945*, Conway Maritime Press, London (1981)
Howarth, David, *The Dreadnoughts*, Time-Life Books, Alexandria, VA (1980)
Jellicoe, John, *The Grand Fleet, 1914–16: Its Creation, Development and Work*, Harvard University Press, Cambridge, MA (1919)
Jellicoe, Nicholas, *Jutland: The Unfinished Battle*, Seaforth Publishing, Barnsley (2016)
Konstam, Angus, *Jutland 1916: Twelve Hours to Win the War*, Aurum Press, London (2016)
Lavery, Brian, *Shield of Empire: The Royal Navy and Scotland*, Birlinn, Edinburgh (2007)
Le Fleming, H. M., *Warships of World War 1(1): Battleships*, Ian Allen, London (1961)
Marder, Arthur J., *From the Dreadnought to Scapa Flow* (5 vols), Oxford University Press, Oxford (1966)
Massie, Robert K., *Dreadnought: Britain, Germany and the Coming of the Great War*, Random House, London (1993)
Moore, John (foreword), *Jane's Fighting Ships of World War 1*, Studio Editions, London (1990)
Parkes, Oscar, *British Battleships, 1860–1950*, Seeley, Service & Co, Sons, London, (1973)
Pears, Randolph, *British Battleships, 1892–1957: The Great Days of the Fleets*, Randolph Pears, London (1957)
Schleihauf, William (ed), *Jutland: The Naval Staff Appreciation*, Seaforth Publishing, Barnsley (2016)
Sondaus, Lawrence, *The Great War at Sea: A Naval History of the First World War*, Cambridge University Press, Cambridge (2014)
Tarrant, V. E., *Jutland: The German Perspective*, Brockhampton Press, London (1995)
Thomas, Roger D. & Patterson, Brian, *Dreadnoughts in Camera, 1905–1920*, Sutton Publishing, Stroud (1998)

INDEX

Page locators in bold refer to captions, plates and pictures.

aircraft **16**, **23**, **24**, 24,**39**
Alexander-Sinclair, Cmdre 63
Arbuthnot, Rear-Adm Sir Robert 37, 65
armour protection 6, 15, 16, 22
armoured cruisers 14, 15, 16, 23, 37, 51, 58, 59, **60**, 66

battle of Dogger Bank 10, 16, 32, **41**, 43, 55, 59
battle of Heligoland Bight, the 16, **41**, 42, 57
battle of Jutland, the 5, 11, **12**, 13, 16, 21, **25**, 32, 39, **41**, 43, 54, 56, **59**, **60**, 62–72, **63**, **64**, **65**, (**65**)**66**, (**69**)**70–71**, 77–78
battle of the Falkland Islands, the 15, 16
battlecruisers 15–16, 19, **19**, 38, 78
Bayly, Vice-Adm Sir Lewis 37
Beatty, Adm Sir David 29, **29**, **32**, **33**, 37, 38–39, 54, 57–58, 59, **60**, 62, 63–64, 65, **65**, 68, 73
Board of Admiralty, the 7–8, 10, 11, **11**, 12, 13, **25**, **26**, 28, 29, **30**, 30–36, 39, 45, 50, 56, 58
First Sea Lord 31, **31**
NID (Naval Intelligence Div) 41–43, 59, 73
Bradford, Vice-Adm Sir Edward 37
British naval strategy 5, 7–8, 10–11, 14, 19, **26**, 26–28, 29, 37–39, 54–55, 56–58, 59, 60, (**60**)**61**, 62, 63–69, (**66**)**67**, (**69**)**70–71**, 73, 76–77, 78
Burney, Vice-Adm Sir Cecil 65, 66, 73

Callaghan, Adm Sir George 32, 36
Carson, Edward 30
ceremonial small-arms drill **31**
Chilean Navy, the **11**, 13
Churchill, Winston 30, 42, 55, 77
coal-fired warships 22, 51, 57
Colville, Vice-Adm Sir Henry 48
conversions and modifications 10, 24, **39**, 47
Cornwall, Boy Seaman 'Jack' **62**
'crossing the T' **67**, 68, 69

deaths and matériel losses 11, 16, 23–24, 45, **58**, 59, **59**, **62**, 63, **64**, 65, 66, 72, 77
destroyers 16–17, 19, 38, 48, 65, **77**
dreadnought battleships 4, **4**, **6**, 6–7, 19, 21, **30**, **33**, 36, 37, (**66**)**67**, 76–77
Iron Duke-class 13, 19, 24, **32**, **43**, **78**
King George V-class 23, **38**, (**51**)**52–53**, **58**
Orion-class dreadnoughts 13, (**51**)**52–53**
Royal Sovereign-class 13, **15**, **31**, 59
Dunning, Sqn Ldr Edwin **23**, 24

economic blockade of Germany, the 5, 7, 11, **25**, 28, 56, 57, 59, 72–73, 76, 77–78
Evan-Thomas, Rear Adm Hugh **13**, 37, 63, 64, 65, 68

fire control systems 6, 19, 20, **38**, **78**
Fisher, Adm Sir John 'Jackie' 30, **30**, 40, 45, 55, 59, 77
fuel oil **20**, 22

Gamble, Vice-Adm Sir Douglas 36, 37
German naval strategy 8, 10, 14, 25–26, 59–60, 62, 63, 65, **66**, 68–69, 72–76
Gefechtskehrtwendung manoeuvre **66**, 68, 69
Kräfteausgleich ('Force Balancing') 10, 28, 77
Risikogedanke ('Risk Theory') 10, 72, 77
German propaganda 56, 72
Goodenough, Cmdre William 37, 54, 57, 58, 59, 64
Gough-Calthorpe, Rear Adm Hon Somerset 37
gun layout 12–13
gunnery direction systems 20–21, 78

Hall, Cmdre Reginald 42, 43
Hamilton, Vice-Adm Sir Frederick 30
Hipper, Vizeadm Franz 58, 59, **60**, 63, 64, 65, 66, 69
Hood, Rear Adm H.L.A. 65
Hope, Cdr Herbert 43
Imperial German Navy, the 7, 8, 77
German High Seas Fleet 8–9, 26–28, 32, 39, 55, 56, 58, 62, 64, 72, 73, 76
surrender 5, **16**, **29**, **38**, **72**, (**73**)**74–75**, 76, 78

German Naval Airship Division 24
Scouting Groups 62, 63, 65
ships
SMS *Blücher* (armoured cruiser) 16, 59
SMS *Derfflinger* (battlecruiser) 63, 66, (**73**)**74–75**
SMS *Elbing* (light cruiser) **11**, 62
SMS *Friedrich der Grosse* (dreadnought) (**73**)**74–75**
SMS *König* (dreadnought) **66**, 68
SMS *Lützow* (battlecruiser) 63, **65**, 72
SMS *Magdeburg* (light cruiser) 42
SMS *Moltke* (battlecruiser) 63, **63**, (**73**)**74–75**, 76
SMS *Seydlitz* (battlecruiser) 63, **63**, (**73**)**74–75**
SMS *Von der Tann* (battlecruiser) 63, (**73**)**74–75**
SMS *Westfalen* (dreadnought) **11**
SMS *Wiesbaden* (light cruiser) 65
U-boats 22, 23–24, 28, 37, 44, 45, 47, **48**, 55, 57, 72
Zeppelin 24, **39**, 44
Ingenohl, Adm Friedrich von 36, 55, 58
intelligence 14, 24, **26**, 31–32, 39, 41–44, 59, 60, 62, 73

Jellicoe, Adm Sir John 4, 5, 11, 14, **25**, 28–29, 30, **31**, 32–33, 36, 39, 40, 41, 43, 45, 46, 50, 51, 54–55, 56–57, 58–59, 60, **60**, 62, 64–65, (**66**)**67**, 66–68, **69**, 69–72, 73, 77, 78
Jerram, Vice-Adm Sir Thomas 62, 66, 68

Lambert, Cmdre Cecil 30
light cruisers 14–15, 19, 38
logistics and supplies 44–45, **50**, 50–51

Madden, Rear Adm Charles E. 32
Mahan, Capt Alfred Thayer 7–8, 10, 11
Influence of Sea Power upon History, The (book) 7
Marine Nationale, the 10
maritime trade routes 7, 8, 28, 76
military strengths 7, 8–10, 14, 58, 59, 77
minefields 22, 23, 26, 47, 51

naval arms race 7, 76, 77
naval aviation sweeps 5, 24, **26**, 38, **51**, 56, 57, 59, 60, 62, **69**, 76
naval bases 44
Cromarty Firth **26**, 39, 45, 46, 54, 55, 58, 59, **60**, 62
Scapa Flow **4**, 5, **7**, **15**, 22, 24, 26, **26**, **31**, 44, 45, 45–51, **46**, **50**, (**51**)**52–53**, **54**, 54–55, 56, 59, 76, 77, **77**
naval defences 45–48, 55
naval exercises **8**, **22**, **58**
North Sea Theatre of Operations (**8**)**9**

observation balloons **43**
obsolescence 6, **6**, 8, **12**, 51
Oliver, Rear Adm Henry 41–42

Pakenham, Vice-Adm William **5**, 58
Pohl, Adm Hugo von 55, 59
propulsion plants 21–22

Queen Elizabeth-class battleships **13**, **20**, **33**, 59

ranges 6, 13, 14, 20, 21, 23, **63**, 65, 66, **66**, 69
recreation and sport 50, **57**, **77**
repairs and maintenance 47, 50, 54, 58, **64**
Rosyth dockyard, Scotland 11, **26**, 36, 38, 44, 51–54, 59, **64**, 73
Royal Australian Navy, the 42
Royal Navy, the 7, 11, 25
Battlecruiser Fleet **5**, 16, 19, **19**, 26, 29, **33**, **36**, 38, 39, 41, 54, 55, 59, 60, **60**, 62, 78
destroyer flotillas 17, **33**, 38, 40, 51, 65
4th Destroyer Flotilla **11**, 65, **77**
Grand Fleet 11, 14, 15, **17–18**, 24, 25, 26, (**26**)**27**, 28, 32, 36, 43, 44, **44**, **46**, **50**, (**51**)**52–53**, **54**, 56, 57, 58, 59, 60, 72, (**73**)**74–75**, 76, 77–78
deployment at sea 1915–16 (**60**)**61**
organisation and structure 33–35, 36–38

Harwich Force **26**, 57–58, 59, 60, 73
Naval Intelligence Div 31–32
ships 10, **11**, **12**, 15, **15**, 23, 24, 45, **47**, 54, 62–63, 64, 65, **77**
HMS *Agincourt* 13, 19
HMS *Audacious* (dreadnought) 23, **58**
HMS *Barham* (battleship) **13**, 64
HMS *Boadicea* (light cruiser) (**51**)**52–53**
HMS *Canada* (dreadnught) 13–14, 19, (**69**)**70–71**
HMS *Cardiff* (light cruiser) (**73**)**74–75**
HMS *Chester* (light cruiser) **62**, 65
HMS *Colossus* **4**, 12
HMS *Conqueror* (dreadnought) **8**, (**51**)**52–53**
HMS *Defence* (armoured cruiser) 66, 72
HMS *Dreadnought* **6**, 6–7, 12, **12**, 21–22, 30
HMS *Erin* (battlecruiser) 13, 19, (**51**)**52–53**
HMS *Furious* (battlecruiser) 10, 19–20, **23**, 24, **39**
HMS *Hood* (battlecruiser) 20, 65
HMS *Indefatigable* (battlecruiser) 16, 63, 72
HMS *Invincible* (battlecruiser) 15, 16, **59**, 66, 72
HMS *Iron Duke* (dreadnought) 32, **32**, 33, 37, **57**, 68, (**69**)**70–71**
HMS *King George V* (dreadnought) **22**, **38**, (**51**)**52–53**, **66**, 68
HMS *Lion* (battlecruiser) **5**, **33**, 38, **41**, 63, 64, 65, **65**
HMS *Marlborough* (dreadnought) **43**, 65, 69, 78
HMS *Monarch* (dreadnought) **8**, (**51**)**52–53**
HMS *Neptune* (dreadnought) **7**, 12
HMS *New Zealand* (battlecruiser) **24**, 63
HMS *Orion* (dreadnought) **8**, 16 (**51**)**52–53**
HMS *Princess Royal* (battlecruiser) **5**, **41**, 63
HMS *Queen Elizabeth* (battleship) 13, **32**
HMS *Queen Mary* (battleship) 16, 42, 63, **63**, 72
HMS *Royal Oak* (dreadnought) **31**, (**69**)**70–71**
HMS *Thunderer* (dreadnought) (**69**)**70–71**
HMS *Tiger* (dreadnought) **5**, 63, **64**
HMS *Warrior* (armoured cruiser) 65, 72
Signals Intelligence 43
squadrons **33**, **60**
1st Battle **12**, 37, 66, (**69**)**70–71**
1st Battlecruiser **33**, 37, **41**, 65–66
1st Light Cruiser 54, 57, 58, 62–63
2nd Battle **8**, 36, 37, 39, (**51**)**52–53**, 55, **58**, 59, 62, 66, (**69**)**70–71**
2nd Battlecruiser 33
2nd Light Cruiser 64
3rd Battle **36**, 37, 51, 54, (**69**)**70–71**
3rd Battlecruiser **33**, 51, **59**, 65
4th Battle **33**, 36, 37, 66
5th Battle **13**, **33**, **60**, 62, 63, 64, 65, 66

Scarborough, Hartlepool and Whitby raids, the 5, 32, 43, 54, 55, 58, 59
Scheer, Vizeadm Reinhard von 55, 60, 65, **66**, 68–69, 72, 73
ship design 13, 15, 16
shipbuilding 11, 13
signal lamps 40–41
speeds 6, 15, 16, 17, 21, 22, 23, 24, 68, 78
Sturdee, Vice-Adm Sir Doveton **12**, 31
submarine attacks 73, 76

Tirpitz, Adm Alfred von **8**, 10, 77

Warrender, Vice-Adm Sir George 37, **51**, 55, 58
weaponry 6, 12, 13, 14, 15–17, 19, 20, 38
2-pdr AA gun (UK) 24
3-pdr 1.85 in. Vickers gun (UK) **45**
13½ in.gun (UK) **22**, 68
15in. Mk I gun (UK) **19**, 20, 59
'Carbonit' contact mine (Germany) 22–23
G/6 torpedo (Germany) 23
self-propelled torpedo (UK) 16, 23
Wilhelm II, Kaiser **8**, 72, 73
wireless communications **26**, 39–41, 43–44, 50, 56, 64, 65, 78